Workbook in
PHYSICAL
ANTHROPOLOGY

4

Workbook in
PHYSICAL
ANTHROPOLOGY
SECOND EDITION

Philip L. Stein
Bruce M. Rowe
Los Angeles Pierce College

McGraw-Hill Book Company
New York/St. Louis/San Francisco/Auckland/Bogotá/Düsseldorf
Johannesburg/London/Madrid/Mexico/Montreal/New Delhi
Panama/Paris/São Paulo/Singapore/Sydney/Tokyo/Toronto

WORKBOOK IN PHYSICAL ANTHROPOLOGY

ISBN 0-07-061119-X

2 3 4 5 6 7 8 9 0 WHWH 7 8 3 2 1 0 9

This book was set in Souvenir Light by Waldman Graphics, Inc. The editors were Lyle Linder, Eric M. Munson, and Laura D. Warner; the designer was Anne Canevari Green; the production supervisor was Dennis J. Conroy. New drawings were done by J & R Services, Inc.
The Whitlock Press, Inc., was printer and binder.

ILLUSTRATION ACKNOWLEDGMENTS

1-1, 1-2, 16-1, 16-2, 16-3, 16-4, 16-5, 27-2, 27-3, 31-1, 31-2, 32-1, 32-2b, 32-3, 32-4, 33-2, 33-3. Photos by Rick Freed.

1-3, 1-4. Photos by Paul A. Meyers.

3-4a, b, c, d, 6-1a, b. Copyright © 1960, 1968, 1969, 1970 by the American Society of Human Genetics. Used by permission of the University of Chicago Press.

3-4e. Courtesy of the *Journal of Medical Genetics* (C. A. Clarke, editor, and the British Medical Association, publisher) and Dr. Tay Chong Hai.

4-1, 4-2, 4-3. Bio-Science Laboratories, Van Nuys, Calif.

4-4, 4-5, 4-6. Courtesy of Norman R. Davidson, Medical Research Council, Edinburgh.

5-1, 5-2, 26-1, 27-1b, 36-2. Carolina Biological Supply Company.

6-1c. Used by permission of The American Genetic Association.

17-1. From Alan C. Swedlund and William D. Wade, *Laboratory Methods in Physical Anthropology* (Prescott, Ariz.: Prescott College Press, 1972.) Used by permission of the Prescott College Press.

19-1. From W. K. Gregory, *Evolution Emerging,* vol. 2 (New York: Macmillan, 1951). Courtesy of The American Museum of Natural History.

23-2. From W. M. Krogman, *The Human Skeleton in Forensic Medicine* (Springfield, Ill.: Charles C Thomas, 1962).

23-3. Copyright by the American Dental Association. Reprinted by permission.

27-1a. San Diego Zoo photos.

32-2a, 33-1, 36-1, 36-2. Photos by Dodie Stoneburner.

Contents

Basic Topics Covered

Relationship of Workbook Exercises to Chapters in Introductory Physical Anthropology Texts*

Exercise	Stein and Rowe, 2d ed.	Jolly and Plog	Weiss and Mann	Lasker, 2d ed.	Birdsell, 2d ed.	Poirier, 2d ed.
1 Human Genetics Survey	3	2	8	4	3	(3)
2 Solving Genetic Problems	3	2	8	(4)	3	(3)
3 Pedigree Analysis	3	(2)	(8)	(4)	(3)	—
4 Karyotyping	4	(2)	8	3	(3)	—
5 Cell Division	4	(2)	8	3	3	4
6 Sex Linkage	4	(2)	8	4	(3)	4
7 Blood Typing	4	12	9, 11	5	16	23
8 Blood Problems	4	12	9, 11	5	16	23
9 Using the Hardy-Weinberg Formula	5	2	8	6	14	20
10 Sampling Error	5	2	9	9	15, 16	20
11 Assortative Mating; Assortative Dating	5	(2)	12	6	14	24
12 Biostatistics	(6)	(2)	(2)	(7)	(15)	(4, 20)
13 Natural Selection	6	2	2	7	15	4, 20
14 Relative Fitness and Selection Coefficients	6	(2)	2	(7)	(15)	(4), 20
15 Statistical Analysis of Phenotypic Variation	7, 8	12	9, (10)	9, 19–21	16–18	20–24
16 Anthropometry	7, 8	(12)	9	19	17	21
17 Dermatoglyphics	(7, 8)	(12)	(9)	4	(17)	(23)
18 Growth and Development	8	(12)	8	9, 20	(17)	(22, 23)
19 The Postcranial Skeleton	12	5	4	15	(10, 11, 12)	15, D

20 The Skull	12	5	4	15	(10, 11, 12)	(15), D
21 Osteometry	12, 14, 15	5, 6, 7	4, 7	15–20	9–12	14–17
22 Sexing Skeletal Material	(12, 14, 15)	(5–8)	(4, 6, 7)	(14–18)	9–12	(14–17)
23 Aging Skeletal Material	8, (12, 14, 15)	(5–8)	(4, 6, 7)	(14–18)	9–12	(14–17)
24 Folk Taxonomy	7, 8	(12)	10	(21)	19	(21)
25 Taxonomy	9	3	2, 4	10	2, 9	2, 5
26 Chordate Structure	9	—	(3)	10	(5)	—
27 The Mammals	9	—	3	10	6	2
28 Observations of Living Primates	10, 11	4, 5	4, 5	11, 12	7, 8	6, 7, 8
29 An Exercise in Observing Primate Behavior	11	4, 5	4, 5	12	8	6, 7, 8
30 Primate Locomotion	12	5	4	11	7, 8	D
31 Comparative Anatomy of the Primate Skeleton	12	5	4	(11)	D	D
32 Comparative Anatomy of the Primate Skull	12	5	4	(15)	D	(10)
33 Comparative Anatomy of Primate Dentition	12	5	4	11	D	10
34 Radiometric Dating	13	6, 8	6, 7	15, 17	4	9
35 Variability in Fossil Populations	14, 15	6, 7, 8	6, 7	14–18	9–12	11–12, 14–17
36 Recognizing Fossil Hominids	14, 15	6, 7, 8	6, 7	15–18	9–12	11–17
37 Osteometry of Fossil Skulls	14, 15	6, 7, 8	6, 7	14–18	9–12	11–12, 14–17

*Chapters refer to the place in the text that either discusses material in the exercise or relates to the general area of the exercise. Parentheses are used to indicate that the topic is not specifically discussed. D indicates that material is dispersed throughout several chapters. A dash indicates that the topic area is not discussed at all in the text.

Preface

The purpose of this workbook is twofold. First, it is an aid to the student of physical anthropology in understanding a number of basic concepts in the areas of human genetics, cytogenetics, population genetics, anthropometry, dermatoglyphics, growth and development, analysis of human skeletal material, taxonomy, primate behavior, comparative anatomy of the living primates, radiometric dating, and human paleontology. Second, it is designed to provide an opportunity to investigate anthropological topics in laboratory and field situations. Merely reading about genetics, primatology, human variation, human paleonotology, and so forth, is often not enough to provide a real understanding, a "feeling" for the subject matter. What is desirable, but often not obtainable, is some type of out-of-class experience in working with the subject itself.

Realizing that laboratory equipment is usually unavailable in an introductory course, we designed this workbook to provide a laboratory-type experience without much in the way of specialized equipment. Photographs show material through the microscope and provide skeletal material for measurement, and so on. Some exercises can be studied with a minimum of unspecialized equipment. Many can easily be converted to laboratory exercises if actual materials such as skeletons and fossil casts are available.

On the basis of responses from our students and other instructors we have made several changes in this edition. Some exercises, which were apparently assigned infrequently, have been eliminated. On the other hand, we have added several new exercises in the areas of blood typing (Exercise 7), phenotypic variation (Exercise 15), sexing and aging skeletal material (Exercises 22 and 23), radiometric dating (Exercise 34), and osteometry of fossil skulls (Exercise 37). Many other exercises have been improved, and a number of illustrations from the first edition have been replaced or changed. The glossary has been enlarged, and many new titles have been added to the Suggested Readings. The table on pages viii and ix correlates the exercises to the major textbooks in physical anthropology. In addition, some notes to the instructor—including accounts of our experiences in using these exercises, suggestions on how to adapt the exercises to laboratory situations, and sources of equipment and supplies—can be found in the *Instructor's Manual for Physical Anthropology: Text and Workbook.*

It is assumed that this workbook will be used in conjunction with a textbook. Therefore, only minimal explanations of basic concepts and principles are provided. Most terms which appear in italics will be found in the glossary at the end of the book. We feel that, with 37 exercises, all instructors will be able to find a selection of material to fit their particular courses. Each of the exercises is a self-contained unit, and they can be assigned in any order.

We would like to take this opportunity to thank all those who have assisted in the preparation of this workbook. First, we wish to thank Rita Castellano and Robert L. Pence, our colleagues at Los Angeles Pierce College, for their help in developing the exercises and trying them out in their classes. Second, we thank Everett and Janet Frost, Vinson Sutlive, Mary Walek, and Karen Kovac for reading the manuscript; Lyle Linder, our editor; Anne Canevari Green, our designer; Laura D. Warner, our editing supervisor; and Dennis J. Conroy, our production supervisor. Finally, a special thanks to Carol Stein for editing and typing, and to Rick Freed and Dodie Stoneburner for the original photography.

Philip L. Stein
Bruce M. Rowe

Workbook in
PHYSICAL ANTHROPOLOGY

Exercise 1

Human Genetics Survey

The term *phenotype* refers to a person's observable or measurable characteristics. A *trait* is simply one aspect of the phenotype. Usually the phenotype results from the interaction of the individual's genetic makeup, or *genotype,* and the environment. However, there are a small number of human traits which do not appear to be affected by the external environment and which occur in a fairly high frequency. These traits can be used to illustrate the basic principles of genetics.

Several traits are described below along with the genetic mechanism involved. On the form on page 7, indicate your phenotype and possible genotypes with respect to each trait. On the form on page 8, summarize the data collected from the class. These data will be saved for use in Exercise 9.

Tongue Rolling   This trait involves the ability to roll your tongue longitudinally into a U shape. Many people are incapable of performing this feat. Although in a few cases practice is necessary for those with the genetic potential to roll their tongues, those who are "nonrollers" are never able to do so. This ability is inherited as a dominant, while those individuals who cannot roll their tongues are *homozygous recessive.*[1]

Tongue Folding   This trait involves the ability to turn the tip of your tongue back upon the main body of the tongue without using the teeth in any way. Like tongue rolling, tongue folding may require some practice among those who have the potential to perform this act. Tongue folding is inherited as a recessive. Therefore, those who

[1]A. H. Sturtevant, "A New Inherited Character in Man," *Proceedings of the National Academy of Sciences,* 26 (1940), 100−102.

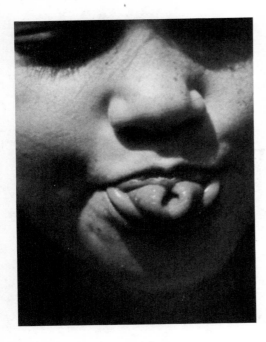

Figure 1-1 Tongue rolling.

can fold their tongues are homozygous recessive.[2] By the way, tongue rolling and tongue folding are inherited independently of one another.[3]

Earlobes Individuals with attached earlobes are characterized by the attachment of the lower part of the ear directly onto the head. Although there may be variations in the shape of the lower part of the ear, a free-hanging lobe is absent. The attached earlobe, or lack of a free-hanging lobe, is inherited as a recessive.[4]

Darwin Tubercle The Darwin tubercle is a projection on the helix of the ear resulting from a thickening of the cartilage of the ear. The actual size of the tubercle varies. The tubercle is inherited as a dominant, but its expression is variable. Some individuals with the dominant allele may show the tubercle on only one ear, and a minority of individuals may not show it at all.[5]

[2]T. C. Hsu, "Tongue Upfolding: A Newly Reported Heritable Character in Man," *Journal of Heredity,* 39 (1948), 187–188.

[3]T. T. Liu and T. C. Hsu, "Tongue-Folding and Tongue-Rolling in a Sample of the Chinese Population," *Journal of Heredity,* 40 (1949), 19–21.

[4]E. F. Powell and D. D. Whitney, "Ear Lobe Inheritance: An Unusual Three-Generation Photographic Pedigree-Chart," *Journal of Heredity,* 28 (1937), 185–186.

[5]T. Quelprud, "Zur Erblichkeit des Darwinschen Höckerchens," *Zeitschrift für Morphologie und Anthropologie,* 34 (1934), 343–363.

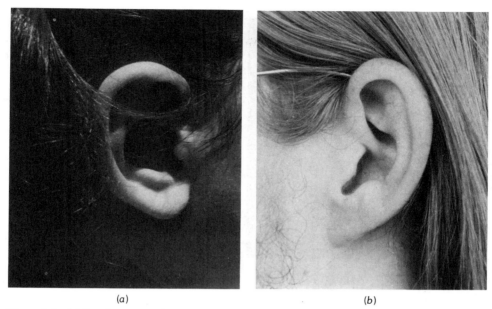

(a)   (b)

Figure 1-2   (a) Free-hanging and (b) attached earlobes.

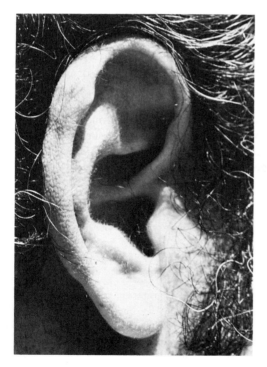

Figure 1-3   Darwin tubercle.

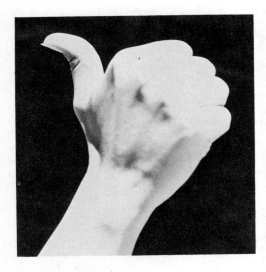

Figure 1-4 Hitchhiker's thumb.

Earwax Earwax, or cerumen, occurs in two basic forms. The dry form is gray and brittle while the wet form is brown and sticky. The dry form is inherited as a recessive.[6]

Hitchhiker's Thumb Put your hand in a hitchhiker's position. Can you bend your thumb back at a sharp angle (50 degrees or greater)? If you can, you have hitchhiker's thumb, or distal hyperextensibility, which is inherited as a recessive.[7]

Mid-Digital Hair Look at the middle segment of all your fingers. Note the presence or absence of hair on this segment. Complete absence of hair indicates a homozygous recessive genotype. It should be noted that sometimes certain types of work may wear the hair away.[8]

PTC Tasting PTC, or phenylthiocarbamide, is a human-made chemical. While the majority of people find PTC to have a bitter taste, many find this substance tasteless. To determine whether or not one is a taster, one need only chew a strip of filter paper which has been soaked in a concentrated solution of PTC. The ability to taste PTC is inherited as a dominant.[9]

[6]E. Matsunaga, "The Dimorphism in Human Normal Cerumen," *Annals of Human Genetics, London,* 25 (1962), 273–286.

[7]B. Glass and J. C. Kistler, "Distal Hyperextensibility of the Thumbs," *Acta Genetica et Statistica Medica,* 4 (1953), 192–206.

[8]M. M. Bernstein and B. S. Burks, "The Incidence and Mendelian Transmission of Mid-Digital Hair in Man," *Journal of Heredity,* 33 (1942), 45–53.

[9]A. L. Fox, "The Relationship between Chemical Constitution and Taste," *Proceedings of the National Academy of Sciences,* 18 (1932), 115–120; and A. F. Blakeslee, "Genetics of Sensory Thresholds: Taste for Phenyl Thio Carbamide," *Proceedings of the National Academy of Sciences,* 18 (1932), 120–130.

Relative Finger Length   Lay your right hand on a piece of lined paper with the fingers perpendicular to the lines. Note the relative lengths of the second (index) and fourth (ring) fingers. There are three possible situations: second finger is longer than the fourth, second finger is shorter than the fourth, or second finger is the same length as the fourth. Those individuals who are homozygous for the allele for short index fingers ($I^S I^S$) will have an index finger which is shorter than the ring finger. Those individuals who are homozygous for the allele for long index finger ($I^L I^L$) will have an index finger which is longer than the ring finger. However, the expression of the two alleles in the *heterozygous* individual shows that this trait is *sex-influenced*. Males with the genotype $I^S I^L$ will have an index finger which is equal to or shorter than the ring finger. But females with the genotype $I^S I^L$ will have an index finger which is equal to or longer than the ring finger.[10]

---

[10]V. R. Phelps, "Relative Finger Length as a Sex-Influenced Trait in Man," *American Journal of Human Genetics*, 4 (1952) 72–89.

Name _____ Class _____ Date _____

Genetic Survey

Trait	Phenotype	Probable Genotype(s)
Tongue rolling	_____	_____
Tongue folding	_____	_____
Earlobes	_____	_____
Darwin tubercle	_____	_____
Earwax	_____	_____
Hitchhiker's thumb	_____	_____
Mid-digital hair	_____	_____
PTC tasting	_____	_____
Relative finger length	_____	_____

Sex _____

Summary of Genetic Data for Class

Trait	N*	No. dom.†	No. rec.‡	%dom.	%rec.
Tongue rolling	_____	_____	_____	_____	_____
Tongue folding	_____	_____	_____	_____	_____
Earlobes	_____	_____	_____	_____	_____
Darwin tubercle	_____	_____	_____	_____	_____
Earwax	_____	_____	_____	_____	_____
Hitchhiker's thumb	_____	_____	_____	_____	_____
Mid-digital hair	_____	_____	_____	_____	_____
PTC tasting	_____	_____	_____	_____	_____
Relative finger length:					
Males	_____	_____	_____	_____	_____
Females	_____	_____	_____	_____	_____

Be sure to save this page for use in Exercise 9.

*N = number of persons in sample.
†dom = dominant trait.
‡ = recessive trait.

Exercise 2

Solving Genetic Problems

This exercise on solving simple genetic problems is designed to provide insight into the principles of Mendelian genetics. This exercise (2) and the one that follows on pedigree analysis (3) illustrate methods used by the genetic counselor in analyzing the inheritance of genetic abnormalities and computing the probability that a specific abnormality with a known mode of inheritance will appear in a particular family.

PROBLEMS

The following is a self-test in the solving of genetic problems. Work each problem in the space provided. Then check your answers with the answers given at the end of this section. Examine the brief explanation to make sure that you did the problems correctly and, more important, that you understood them. If you worked the problems incorrectly or if you do not understand them, mark an X in the space beside the problem number. Then follow the instructions found at the end of this section.

_____ **1.** *PTC tasting* is the ability to taste the harmless substance phenylthiocarb-amide, which is inherited as a dominant *allele* (see Exercise 1). Persons who cannot taste this substance are homozygous recessive. A man is able to taste PTC. His father is a taster, but his mother is a nontaster. The man's wife is also a nontaster. What type of children would be expected to result from this marriage? In what frequencies?

_____ **2.** *Chondrodystrophic dwarfism* is the result of the inheritance of a dominant allele. A dwarf whose father is a dwarf but whose mother is normal marries a normal woman. What is the probability of their having a child who is a chondrodystrophic dwarf?

_____ **3.** A woman is heterozygous for PTC tasting and *tongue rolling.* Her husband cannot taste PTC, nor can he roll his tongue. What phenotypes would be expected to be found among their children and in what proportions?

ANSWERS AND DISCUSSIONS

1. The ability to taste PTC is inherited as a dominant allele. The man, who is a taster, must carry at least one allele for tasting. His mother is a nontaster, *tt*. He could have inherited a recessive allele, *t,* only from his mother. Since he is a taster, he must have inherited a *T* from his father. He is therefore heterozygous, *Tt*. His wife is a nontaster, *tt*. The mating can be written as follows: *Tt* × *tt*. The father can pass on to his children either the *T* or the *t.* One-half of his children would get the *T* and one-half the *t.* All the children would inherit the *t* from the mother. The two probabilities among the children are ½ *Tt* and ½ *tt*. In phenotypic terms, one-half would be expected to be tasters and one-half nontasters.

2. The dwarf possesses the dominant allele, *D*. But since his mother is normal, *dd,* he must have inherited a *d* from her. His genotype is therefore *Dd*. The mating can be written as follows: *Dd* × *dd*. While all the children would inherit the recessive allele, *d,* from the mother, the children can inherit either the *D* or the *d* from the father. One-half will inherit the *D* and be dwarfs, while the other half will inherit the *d* and be normal. The probability of a child's being born a dwarf is therefore ½.

3. This is a problem in *independent assortment.* The woman is heterozygous for both traits. Her genotype can be written as *TtRr*. Her husband is a nontaster and a nonroller. These are both homozygous recessive traits. His genotype can be written as *ttrr*. The mating can be written as follows: *TtRr* × *ttrr*. According to the principle of independent assortment, the inheritance of PTC tasting is independent of the inheritance of tongue rolling. We can therefore divide this problem into two parts. First, we must find the results of the mating *Tt* × *tt*. We obtain the answer ½ *Tt* (taster) and ½ *tt* (nontaster). Second, we must find the results of the mating *Rr* × *rr*. We obtain the answer ½ *Rr* (roller) and ½ *rr* (nonroller). To complete the problem, we make use of one of the laws of probability which states that the probability of the occurrence of two independent events is the product of the individual probabilities.

The four possible combinations and the probabilities of each are: (a) taster and roller, $\frac{1}{2} \times \frac{1}{2} = \frac{1}{4}$; (b) taster and nonroller, $\frac{1}{2} \times \frac{1}{2} = \frac{1}{4}$; (c) nontaster and roller, $\frac{1}{2} \times \frac{1}{2} = \frac{1}{4}$; (d) nontaster and nonroller, $\frac{1}{2} \times \frac{1}{2} = \frac{1}{4}$.

INSTRUCTIONS

If you missed problem 1, go to section A.

If you missed problem 2, go to section B.

If you missed problem 3, go to section C.

If you answered all questions correctly, or after you have worked through sections A, B, and/or C, go to section D.

SECTION A: PROBLEMS

In the following series of problems, we shall use PTC tasting as our example. Answer the following questions. The answer and explanation for each question are given at the end of this section.

1. Two taster parents produced both taster and nontaster children. Reconstruct the genotypes of the parents.

2. Why do matings between two nontaster parents produce nontaster children only?

3. In a genetic survey of the offspring of two tasters, tasters as well as nontasters were noted. Explain why tasters can produce nontaster children. Why will some matings between two tasters never produce nontaster children?

4. If two tasters, both heterozygous for the trait, mate, what types would appear among their children? Give genotypes and phenotypes.

5. In the above problem, what proportion of the children would be expected to be tasters? Nontasters?

6. If a heterozygous taster mated with a nontaster, what proportion of the children would be expected to be tasters? Nontasters?

7. If a homozygous taster mated with a nontaster, what would be the probability of having a nontaster child? A taster child?

ANSWERS AND DISCUSSIONS

1. Since a nontaster child is *tt*, each parent must carry a *t*. Since the parents are tasters, they must also carry a *T*. They are therefore heterozygous *Tt*.

2. Nontasters are homozygous recessive, *tt*. They produce *sex cells* that carry the *t* only. Therefore, all children will receive a *t* from each parent and will be *tt*, or nontasters. This is the only possibility.

3. All tasters must carry at least one dominant allele, *T*. However, if the two persons are heterozygous, *Tt*, then they can produce some nontaster children who receive the *t* from each. Of course, if either or both tasters are homozygous dominant, *TT*, then no nontaster children will be produced.

4. The mating can be written as follows: *Tt* × *Tt*. The first parent will provide either a *T* or a *t* allele. The same is true of the second parent. There are four possibilities. The child could receive (*a*) the *T* from the first parent and the *T* from the second, (*b*) the *T* from the first parent and the *t* from the second, (*c*) the *t* from the first parent and the *T* from the second, and (*d*) the *t* from the first parent and the *t* from the second. The offspring will therefore have the following genotypes: *TT, Tt, tT,* and *tt*. The first three genotypes result in the ability to taste PTC, while the fourth does not. Both taster and nontaster children can be produced.

5. The probability of inheriting the *T* from either parent is ½, since we are dealing with one of two possibilities. The same is true of the inheritance of the *t*. The probability of inheriting a *T* from both parents is ½ × ½ = ¼. The probability of inheriting a *t* from both parents is ½ × ½ = ¼. What we are doing is simply multiplying the individual probabilities. The probability of inheriting the *T* from the first parent and the *t* from the second is also ½ × ½ = ¼. This is also true for the combination *tT*. Since the combination *Tt* is the same as *tT*, we can say that the probability of inheriting one *T* and one *t*, without specifying which allele comes from which parent, is ¼ + ¼ = ½. Here we simply add the two cases. The proportion of taster children is the proportion of *TT* plus *Tt* children, or ¼ + ½ = ¾. The only nontaster children will be those with the genotype *tt*. The probability of inheriting two *t* alleles is ¼.

6. The mating can be written as follows: *Tt* × *tt*. The offspring will inherit either the *T* or the *t* from the first parent (with a probability of ½ for each). The offspring will definitely inherit the *t* from the second parent. There is no other possibility. Therefore, we can state that the probability of receiving the *t* from the second parent is 1. The probability of receiving the *T* from the first parent and the *t* from the second is ½ × 1 = ½, and the probability of receiving the *t* from the first parent and the *t* from the second is ½ × 1 = ½. The probability of having a nontaster child is ½, and a taster child ½.

7. The mating can be written as follows: *TT* × *tt*. The probability of inheriting the *T* from the first parent is 1, and the probability of inheriting the *t* from the second parent is also 1. Therefore, the probability of the child's being a taster, *Tt*, is 1 × 1 = 1, or certainty. The probability of the child's being a nontaster is 0.

SECTION B: PROBLEMS
In the following series of problems, we will use brachydactyly as an example of a trait which is inherited as a dominant. *Brachydactyly* is a skeletal abnormality resulting in unusually short fingers. Attempt to answer the following questions. The answer and explanation for each question are given at the end of this section.

1. A man with brachydactyly mates with a woman with normal fingers. The first child inherits the abnormality. What is this child's genotype?

2. In a genetic survey of families with brachydactylous individuals, it was noted that all brachydactylous people have at least one parent with the abnormality. Explain.

3. Why do not two normal parents produce brachydactylous children?

4. A brachydactylous woman (heterozygous) mates with a normal man. Could they have brachydactylous children? What proportion of the children would be expected to have the trait?

5. A brachydactylous man (homozygous) mates with a normal woman. Could they have brachydactylous children? What proportion of the children would be expected to have the trait?

6. A brachydactylous man (heterozygous) mates with a woman who also has the trait (heterozygous). What is the probability of their having a normal child?

ANSWERS AND DISCUSSIONS

1. The brachydactylous child could have inherited a *b* only from the mother, who is normal *bb*. The *B* must have been inherited from the father. The child's genotype is *Bb*.

2. Brachydactyly is inherited as a dominant allele. Brachydactylous individuals are either homozygous *BB* or heterozygous *Bb*. Normal individuals are homozygous recessive, *bb*. In this situation there are no carriers. Whenever the *B* allele occurs, the trait is expressed. Since all individuals with this abnormality must have inherited a *B* from one of the parents, this parent must also show the trait.

3. A normal individual has the genotype *bb*. A mating between two normal individuals, *bb* × *bb*, can produce normal children only.

4. This mating can be written as follows: *Bb* × *bb*. All children who inherit the *B* from the mother will have the trait. One-half of the children will inherit the *B*.

5. This mating can be written as follows: *BB* × *bb*. All the children will inherit the *B* from the father and have the defect.

6. This mating can be written as follows: *Bb* × *Bb*. The probability of inheriting the *B* from the father is ½. The same is true for inheritance from the mother. There are four possible combinations which will occur in equal frequencies: *BB, Bb, bB,* and *bb*. The first three will all show the trait. Therefore, the probability that the child will be brachydactylous is ¾, while the probability that the child will be normal is ¼.

SECTION C: PROBLEMS

In the following series of problems, we will use tongue rolling and *attached earlobes* as examples. These traits are described in Exercise 1. Attempt to answer the following questions. The answer and explanation for each question are given at the end of this section.

1. A man and his mate can roll their tongues. However, each has a parent who cannot. Would their children be able to accomplish this feat? What is the probability?

2. A man has free-hanging earlobes. However, his mother and his mate have attached earlobes. Describe the earlobes expected of his children. Indicate the probabilities of the different types.

Solving Genetic Problems

3. A woman can roll her tongue and has free-hanging earlobes. Her father and her mate cannot roll their tongues and have attached earlobes. List the types of children they could produce and the proportions of the different types.

4. A woman is heterozygous for tongue rolling and has attached earlobes. Her mate also is heterozygous for tongue rolling and has free-hanging earlobes (heterozygous). List the types of children they could produce and the expected proportions of the different types.

ANSWERS AND DISCUSSIONS

1. Tongue rolling is inherited as a dominant allele. The nonrolling grandparents must be homozygous recessive, *rr*. Since the parents both inherited an *r* from their parents, each must be *Rr*. The mating can be written as follows: *Rr* × *Rr*. The probability that an offspring will be able to roll its tongue is ¾ (*RR, Rr, rR*).

2. This problem's mating (dealing with earlobes) can be written as follows: *Ee* × *ee*. The probability that the offspring will possess free-hanging earlobes (*Ee*) is ½ and attached earlobes (*ee*) is ½.

3. In this problem we combine the traits of problems 1 and 2. The mating can be written as follows: *RrEe* × *rree*. According to the principle of independent assortment, we know that the inheritance of these two traits is two independent events. We also know that the probability of the occurrence of two independent events is their product. From the previous problems, we know the probabilities for each trait. Combining the two traits, we find the following four types, along with the probabilities: (*a*) can roll tongue and has free-hanging earlobes, ½ × ½ = ¼; (*b*) can roll tongue and has attached earlobes, ½ × ½ = ¼; (*c*) cannot roll tongue and has free-hanging earlobes, ½ × ½ = ¼; and (*d*) cannot roll tongue and has attached earlobes, ½ × ½ = ¼.

4. The mating can be written as follows: *Rree* × *RrEe*. We separate the problem into two parts. In the first part, we have the mating *Rr* × *Rr*. This mating will produce ¾ offspring who can roll their tongues and ¼ who cannot. The second part of the mating is *ee* × *Ee*. This mating will produce ½ offspring with free-hanging earlobes and ½ with attached earlobes. The types of children and their proportions are: (*a*) can roll tongue and has free-hanging earlobes, ¾ × ½ = ⅜; (*b*) can roll tongue and has attached earlobes, ¾ × ½ = ⅜; (*c*) cannot roll tongue and has free-hanging earlobes, ¼ × ½ = ⅛; and (*d*) cannot roll tongue and has attached earlobes, ¼ × ½ = ⅛.

SECTION D: PROBLEMS

1. A couple has a child with *alkaptonuria*. The parents are normal. What is the probability that the next child will also have this defect?

2. In the above problem, what is the probability of having three children, all with the disease?

3. The heterozygote for the sickle-cell allele is said to have the *sickle-cell trait*. If two persons with the sickle-cell trait were to mate, what would be the probability of their having a child with *sickle-cell anemia*?

4. In the above problem, what is the probability of having a child with the sickle-cell trait?

5. Two normal parents have an *albino* child. The child grows up and marries another albino. What proportion of their children would be expected to be albino?

6. An albino marries a known carrier for albinism. What is the probability of their having an albino child?

7. Two first cousins want to marry and have children, but they are worried because they have an albino grandfather in common. What is the probability that this couple will have an albino child? Assume that everyone is homozygous dominant unless there is evidence to the contrary.

8. *Huntington's chorea* is inherited as a dominant. If a woman with the defect (assume she is heterozygous) mates with a normal man, what is the probability of their having a normal child?

9. In the above problem, what is the probability of their having two normal children?

10. Chondrodystrophic dwarfism is inherited as a dominant. If two heterozygous dwarfs married, what proportion of their offspring would be expected to be dwarfs?

11. If a heterozygous dwarf married a normal individual, what proportion of their offspring would be expected to be dwarfs?

12. In Exercise 1 we saw that tongue rolling is inherited as a dominant while tongue folding is inherited as a recessive. A woman and a man, both heterozygous for tongue rolling and the inability to fold the tongue, mate. Describe the children which could be produced and the probabilities.

13. A man can taste PTC, can roll his tongue, and has *free-hanging earlobes*. He is heterozygous for all three. His mate cannot taste PTC, cannot roll her tongue, and has attached earlobes. Describe all types of children which could be produced and their expected proportions.

ANSWERS

1.	¼	**7.**	$^1/_{16}$
2.	$^1/_{64}$	**8.**	½
3.	¼	**9.**	¼
4.	½	**10.**	¾
5.	1	**11.**	½
6.	½		

12. $^9/_{16}$ rolling, nonfolding; $^3/_{16}$ rolling, folding; $^3/_{16}$ nonrolling, nonfolding; $^1/_{16}$ nonrolling, folding.

13.

PTC Tasting	Tongue Rolling	Free-Hanging Earlobes	
+	+	+	⅛
+	+	−	⅛
+	−	+	⅛
+	−	−	⅛
−	+	+	⅛
−	+	−	⅛
−	−	+	⅛
−	−	−	⅛

SUGGESTED READINGS

Baldwin, R. E. *Genetics.* New York: Wiley, 1973.

Goldstein, P. *Genetics Is Easy.* 4th ed. New York: Viking, 1967.

Stansfield, W. D. *Schaum's Outline of Theory and Problems of Genetics.* New York: McGraw-Hill, 1969.

Vegotsky, A., and C. A. White. *A Programmed Approach to Human Genetics.* New York: Wiley, 1974.

Exercise 3

Pedigree Analysis

While the experimental method is the main approach to genetic studies in nonhuman organisms, the study of human genetics is based to a large extent on the analysis of *pedigrees*. Pedigrees are reconstructions of family groups showing the distribution patterns of particular traits within the group. From these data the geneticist is often able to determine the mode of inheritance. He or she may also be able to reconstruct many individual genotypes and predict the possible results of future matings.

A pedigree (see Figure 3-1) is normally built around an individual who comes to the attention of the doctor or geneticist. This individual is called the *proband* and often is indicated in the pedigree by an arrow (*a*).

A male is indicated by a square (*b*) and a female by a circle (*c*). A mating is indicated by a horizontal line (*d*), with the male on the left. Double lines are used to indicate a *consanguineous mating* (*e*), that is, a mating between biological relatives. A vertical line indicates *descent* (*f*). Children are listed in chronological order, from eldest to youngest, from left to right.

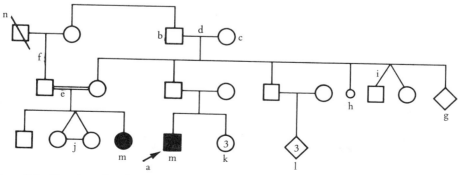

Figure 3-1 Hypothetical pedigree.

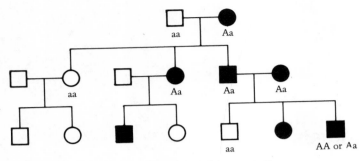

Figure 3-2 Inheritance of a hypothetical dominant trait.

Persons of unknown sex are indicated by a diamond (g). Abortions or stillborns are shown as small circles or squares (h). Twins are indicated by descent lines from a common point (i); a horizontal line indicates *monozygotic* (identical) *twins* (j). To simplify a pedigree, a group of normal siblings may be indicated by a square or circle with the number of individuals indicated (k). A diamond would be used if the sexes are mixed or unknown (l).

Individuals carrying the trait in question are indicated by blackened symbols (m). If more than one trait is being studied, various other notations can be used. A key is then provided. Deceased individuals are often indicated by a line drawn through that individual's symbol (n).

From the pedigree, we may be able to determine whether the trait is inherited as a dominant or a recessive. Figure 3-2 shows a pedigree of a hypothetical dominant trait. Note that in the case of dominant inheritance, an individual with the trait must have at least one parent who also has the trait. Therefore, the trait will occur in all generations that precede any individual with the trait. Of course, a person with the trait can be homozygous or heterozygous for that trait. A normal individual would be homozygous recessive. A child with the trait, with one normal parent, would have to be heterozygous, since he or she must have received the normal recessive allele from that parent. Several genotypes have been reconstructed in Figure 3-2.

Figure 3-3 shows a pedigree of a hypothetical recessive trait. In this case, the affected individual is homozygous recessive. Note that often both parents phenotypically lack the trait. Therefore, they must be carriers. Note that the trait is not found in every generation.

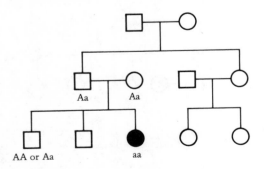

Figure 3-3 Inheritance of a hypothetical recessive trait.

PROBLEMS

The following is a series of pedigrees from the medical literature. On the line underneath each one, indicate whether the trait is inherited as a dominant or a recessive. Also, give the genotype or probable genotypes of the individuals indicated. The traits involved, and the answers, are given at the end of the exercise.

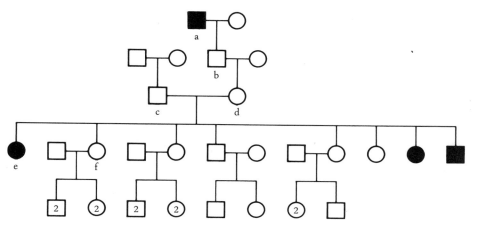

Figure 3-4a   Pedigree A.

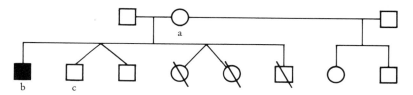

Figure 3-4b   Pedigree B.

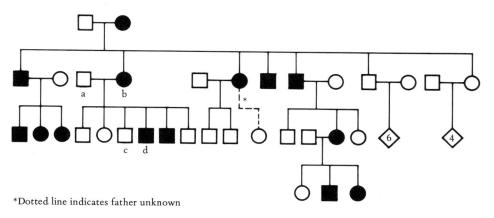

*Dotted line indicates father unknown

Figure 3-4c   Pedigree C.

24

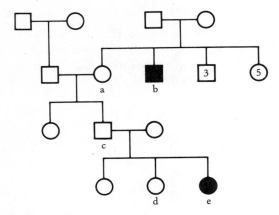

Figure 3-4d Pedigree D.

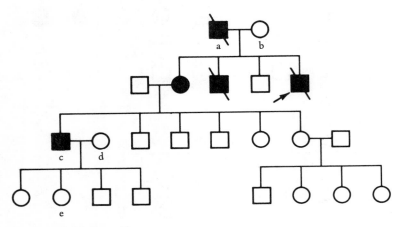

Figure 3-4e Pedigree E.

ANSWERS

A. Recessive, (a) aa, (b) Aa, (c) Aa, (d) Aa, (e) aa, (f) AA or Aa

B. Recessive, (a) Aa, (b) aa, (c) AA or Aa

C. Dominant, (a) aa, (b) Aa, (c) aa, (d) Aa

D. Recessive, (a) Aa, (b) aa, (c) Aa, (d) AA or Aa, (e) aa

E. Dominant, (a) Aa, (b) aa, (c) Aa, (d) aa, (e) aa

(Although Pedigree E is a known dominant, the pedigree could be interpreted as a common recessive: (a) aa, (b) Aa, (c) aa, (d) AA or Aa, (e) Aa. This points out the fact that pedigree analysis can be extremely difficult.)

These pedigrees are actual published pedigrees of (A) albinism, (B) phenylketonuria, (C) congenital aniridia, (D) retinoblastoma, and (E) Huntington's chorea. These abnormalities are defined in the glossary. The pedigrees were published in the following articles:

Exercise 3

A. C. J. Witkop, Jr., et al., "Autosomal Recessive Oculocutaneous Albinism in Man: Evidence for Genetic Heterogeneity," *American Journal of Human Genetics,* 22 (1970), 59.

B. J. H. Renwick et al., "Phenylketonuria: A Linkage Study Using Phenylalanine Tolerance" Tests," *American Journal of Human Genetics,* 22 (1970), 293.

C. M. W. Shaw et al., "Congenital Aniridia," *American Journal of Human Genetics,* 12 (1960), 395.

D. M. T. Macklin, "A Study of Retinoblastoma in Ohio," *American Journal of Human Genetics,* 12 (1960), 35.

E. C. H. Tay, "Huntington's Chorea: Report of a Chinese Family in Singapore," *Journal of Medical Genetics,* 7 (1970), 41.

Exercise 4

Karyotyping

The *chromosomes* provide the key to many of the mechanisms of genetics. Different types of animals are characterized by specific numbers of chromosomes. In humans there are normally forty-six. However, on occasion an individual is born with an abnormal chromosome number or a structural defect in one or more of the chromosomes. Through an examination of microscopic pictures of these bodies, one can discover *chromosome aberrations* which often lead to phenotypic abnormalities.

A *karyotype* is a standardized arrangement of chromosomes. A completed karyotype is shown in Figure 4-1. On the following pages, you will find photographs of human chromosomes as they appear under the microscope. From these, you will prepare karyotypes.

SECTION A: PROBLEMS

To prepare a karyotype, carefully cut out each chromosome from one of the photographs of human chromosomes on pages 29 and 31 and lay them on a piece of paper. Next, arrange the chromosomes into the appropriate groups (A to G) described below. These groups are distinguishable by (1) the size of the chromosome and (2) the position of the *centromere*. Centromere positions are *median* (approximately in the center), *submedian* (off center), and *subterminal* (toward one end). Although the three chromosome pairs of group A can be distinguished, the chromosomes within the other six groups cannot always be distinguished as pairs without the use of some highly specialized techniques (see problems in Section B). The seven groups are:

Group A   This group contains the three longest pairs. The centromeres are median and submedian.

Group B   This group contains two pairs of fairly long chromosomes with submedian centromeres.

Group C   This group consists of seven pairs plus the X *chromosomes*. They are of medium size with median or submedian centromeres.

Group D Within this group are three pairs of chromosomes. They are medium in size with subterminal centromeres.

Group E This group consists of three pairs of small chromosomes with median or submedian centromeres.

Group F This group contains two pairs of small chromosomes with median centromeres.

Group G This group contains two pairs of chromosomes plus the *Y chromosome.* They are small with subterminal centromeres.

After you have sorted out the chromosomes, use the forms on pages 33 and 35 and group the chromosomes in the manner shown in the completed normal female karyotype in Figure 4-1. Remember, within each group it is often impossible to identify individual pairs, except in group A and sometimes in groups D and E. Also, look for some type of abnormality. The individual you are karyotyping may have an abnormal chromosome number or some type of abnormal chromosome structure.

After the chromosomes are lined up by group and number, glue or tape them down. Then, with the aid of the completed karyotype, answer the following questions on the back of each karyotype:

1. How many chromosomes are present?
2. Is this the normal number?
3. What is the sex chromosome count? Is this a normal count?
4. What is the sex of the individual?
5. Are any abnormal chromosomes present?
6. Is this a normal karyotype? If not, summarize all abnormalities noted.

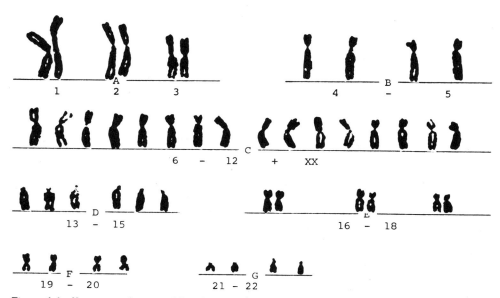

Figure 4-1 Karyotype of a normal female.

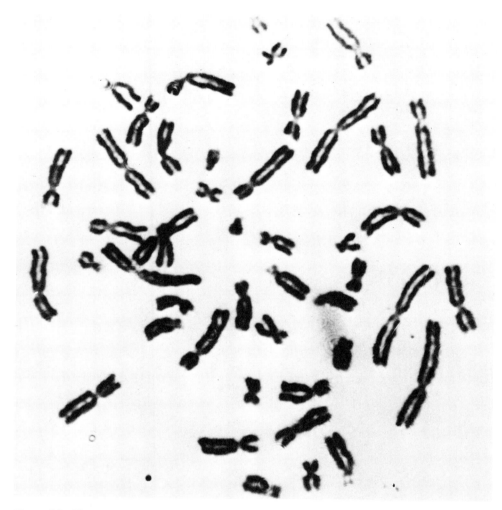

Figure 4-2 Human chromosomes, set 1.

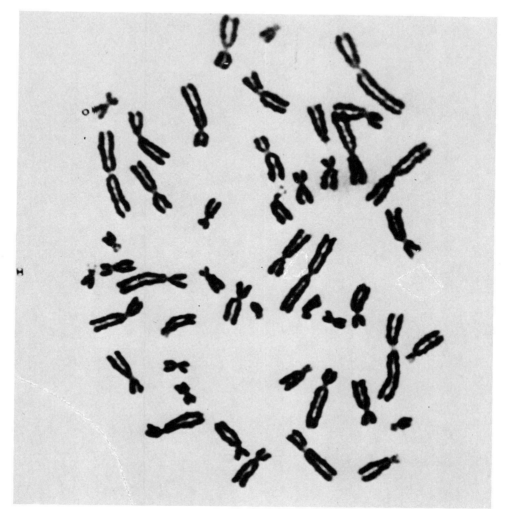

Figure 4-3 Human chromosomes, set 2.

Name ———————————————— Class ——————————— Date ———————

Karyotype Set 1

A (1–3)

B (4–5)

C (6–12, X)

D (13–15)

E (16–18)

F (19–20)

G (21–22, Y)

Answer questions on the back of this page.

33

Karyotype Set 1

1. How many chromosomes are present?

2. Is this the normal number?

3. What is the sex chromosome count? Is this a normal count?

4. What is the sex of the individual?

5. Are any abnormal chromosomes present?

6. Is this a normal karyotype? If not, summarize all abnormalities noted.

Name _____ Class _____ Date _____

Karyotype Set 2

A (1–3)

B (4–5)

C (6–12, X)

D (13–15)

E (16–18)

F (19–20)

G (21–22, Y)

Answer questions on the back of this page.

Karyotype Set 2

1. How many chromosomes are present?

2. Is this the normal number?

3. What is the sex chromosome count? Is this a normal count?

4. What is the sex of the individual?

5. Are any abnormal chromosomes present?

6. Is this a normal karyotype? If not, summarize all abnormalities noted.

SECTION B: PROBLEMS

There are now available a number of techniques which result in a banding pattern on the chromosomes. These techniques, which include *giemsa staining,* permit the identification of each and every chromosome within each group and the precise matching of homologous chromosomes into pairs. Identification of specific bands makes it relatively easy to note small deletions or other rearrangements of the chromosomal material. Figure 4-4 shows a completed karyotype of a normal female and a normal male using a banding technique. Figures 4-5 and 4-6 show chromosome spreads as they appear under the microscope. Using these spreads, prepare karyotypes, following the instructions in Section A. Use the completed karyotypes in Figure 4-4 to aid in the identification of specific chromosomes. Answer the same questions which were asked for the previous karyotypes.

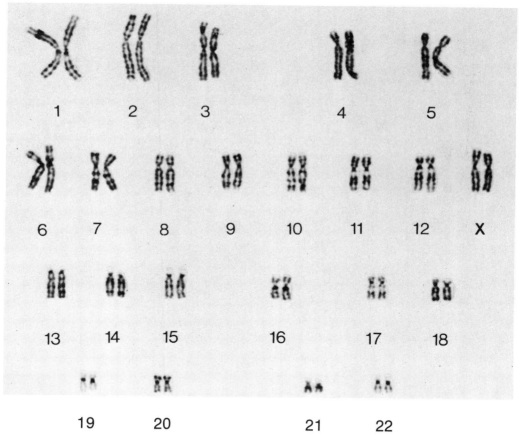

Figure 4-4a   Karyotype of a normal female.

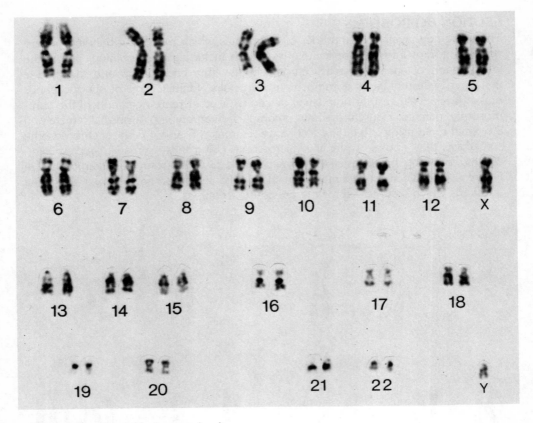

Figure 4-4b Karyotype of a normal male.

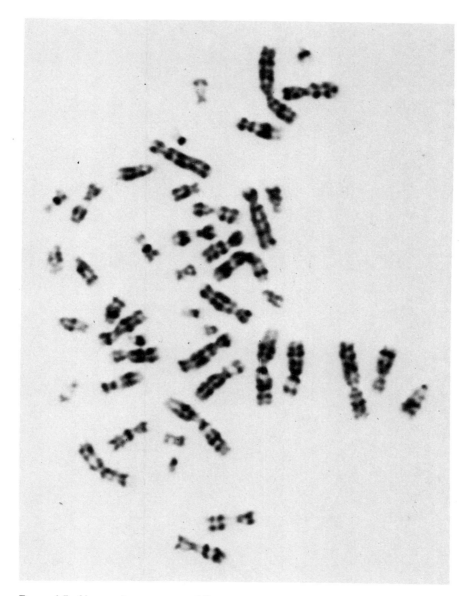

Figure 4-5 Human chromosomes, set 3.

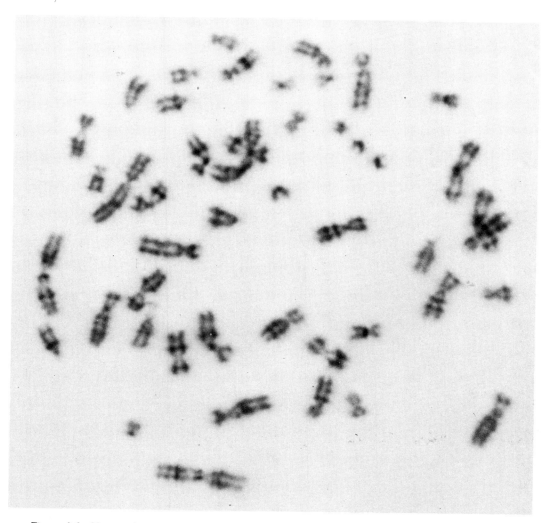

Figure 4-6 Human chromosomes, set 4.

Name _____ Class _____ Date _____

Karyotype Set 3

A (1–3)

B (4–5)

C (6–12, X)

D (13–15)

E (16–18)

F (19–20)

G (21–22, Y)

Answer questions on the back of this page.

43

Karyotype Set 3

1. How many chromosomes are present?

2. Is this the normal number?

3. What is the sex chromosome count? Is this a normal count?

4. What is the sex of the individual?

5. Are any abnormal chromosomes present?

6. Is this a normal karyotype? If not, summarize all abnormalities noted.

Karyotype Set 4

A (1–3)

B (4–5)

C (6–12, X)

D (13–15)

E (16–18)

F (19–20)

G (21–22, Y)

Answer questions on the back of this page.

Karyotype Set 4

1. How many chromosomes are present?

2. Is this the normal number?

3. What is the sex chromosome count? Is this a normal count?

4. What is the sex of the individual?

5. Are any abnormal chromosomes present?

6. Is this a normal karyotype? If not, summarize all abnormalities noted.

ANSWERS

Set 1. This is a normal karyotype of a male. There are forty-six chromosomes. The X chromosome will be one of the C group and the Y chromosome will be one of the G group.

Set 2. This is a karyotype of a female with Down's syndrome. There are forty-seven chromosomes. The two X chromosomes will be found in the C group. The fifth G chromosome is *not* the Y but an extra number 21.

Set 3. This is a karyotype of a normal male. Note the distinctive banding patterns of the X and Y chromosomes which distinguish them from other C and G chromosomes, respectively.

Set 4. This is a karyotype of a male with Down's syndrome. Compare this karyotype with the one you made from set 2.

SUGGESTED READINGS

Ford, E. H. R. *Human Chromosomes.* London: Academic, 1973.

Hamerton, J. L. *Human Cytogenetics.* 2 vols. New York: Academic, 1971.

Exercise 5

Cell Division

It is through an examination of cell division that the physical basis for the Mendelian principles, as well as the exceptions to those principles, become clear. This exercise deals with *mitosis,* the means by which one-celled organisms reproduce and multi-cellular organisms grow and replace body cells, and *meiosis,* the production of sex cells for sexual reproduction.

MITOSIS

Mitosis is the term used to indicate the division of chromosomes in *somatic* cell division. Mitosis can be arbitrarily divided into a series of stages, as follows:

Interphase   A cell in interphase is not dividing. Therefore, we cannot consider this a mitotic stage. In interphase the chromosomes are not visible, although the chromosomal material, the *chromatin,* can be seen as diffuse granular material within the nucleus.

Prophase   Several events occur in prophase as mitosis gets underway. First, the nuclear membrane disappears. Second, the small *centriole,* seen on the outside surface of the nucleus, divides, and each of the two new centrioles moves around until they come to lie at opposite ends of the cell. Third, the *chromosomes* become visible as double-stranded structures composed of two *chromatids* held together by the *centromere.* Although centrioles cannot be seen in the photographs in this exercise, the *spindle fibers,* which can be seen, are radiating out from them.

Metaphase   In metaphase each chromosome lines up on the equatorial plate of the cell, which is defined by the polar position of the centrioles. Fibers radiating out from the centrioles form the spindle which attaches to the centromeres, each centromere having divided.

Anaphase   In anaphase the centromeres are pulled apart, taking their respective chromatids along with them.

Telophase   The final stage in mitosis is telophase. Here, actual cell division takes place, the nuclear membrane reappears, and the chromosomes disappear from view. Mitosis is now complete as interphase begins again.

PROBLEM

The photographs in Figure 5-1 show cells in the process of mitotic division. These cells are from a cross section of the *blastula* (an early embryonic stage) of the whitefish.

Identify the stage of mitosis shown in each photograph:

Photograph	Stage
(a)	
(b)	
(c)	
(d)	

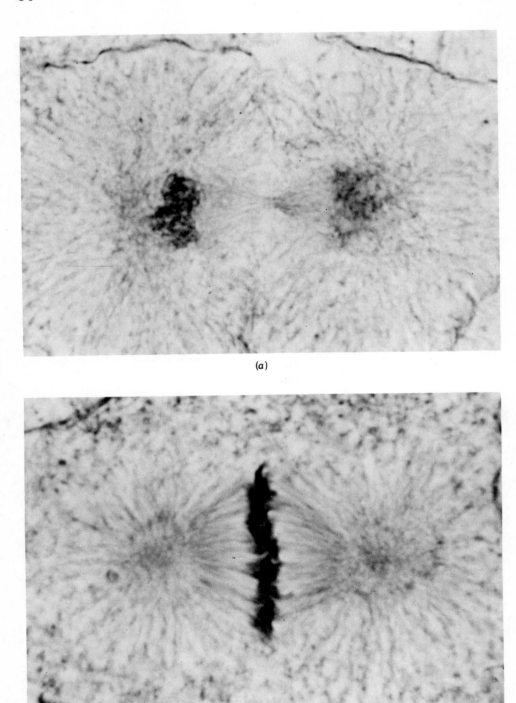

(a)

(b)

Figure 5-1 Stages of mitosis.

Exercise 5

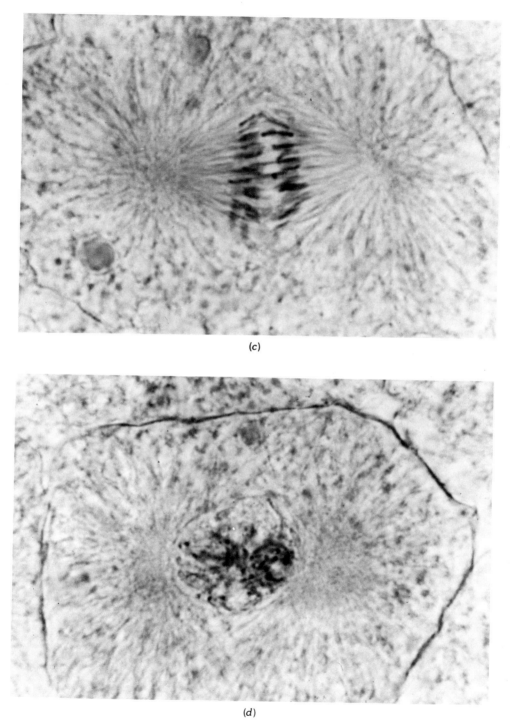

(c)

(d)

Figure 5-1 (*Continued*)

ANSWERS

a Telophase

b Metaphase

c Anaphase

d Prophase

MEIOSIS

Meiosis refers to the behavior of the chromosomes in cell division leading to the production of *sex cells, the sperm* and *ovum* (egg). Our example is a parasitic round-worm, *Ascaris megalocephala,* which is found in pork. In *Ascaris* the ovum does not complete meiotic division until after it has been fertilized.

Figure 5-2*a* shows the metaphase of the first meiotic division. The four chromosomes have come together as two pairs. Unlike mitosis, when the chromosomes line up along the equatorial plane, in the production of ova they line up on one side of the cell. (In the production of sperm the chromosomes line up across the equatorial plane, as in mitosis.)

Figure 5-2*b* shows the telophase of the first meiotic division. The cell is dividing unevenly, with the vast bulk of the cytoplasm going to one of the new cells.

Figure 5-2 Stages of meiosis.

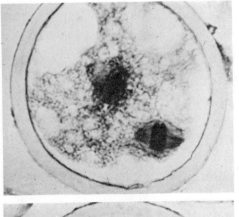

(a)

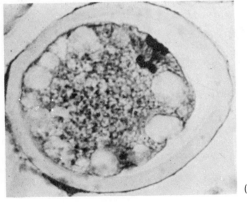

(b)

At the end of telophase, the smaller of the two parts is extruded from the larger cell as a small *polar body* (Figure 5-2c).

Figure 5-2d shows the metaphase of the second division of meiosis. Again, division is uneven.

In Figure 5-2e the second division is completed, forming a second polar body and leaving one large ovum.

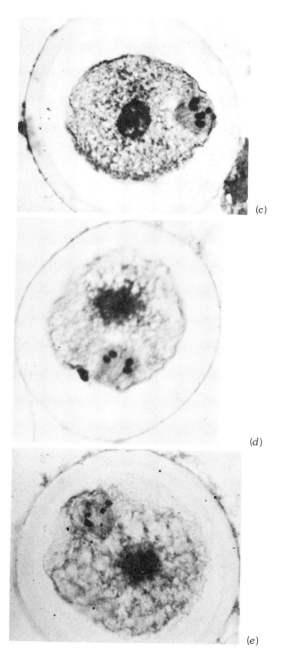

(c)

(d)

(e)

PROBLEMS

1. In what ways does meiosis differ from mitosis?

2. In meiosis, how is the chromosome number reduced from the *diploid* (2n) number to the *haploid* (n) number?

3. How does the second meiotic division differ from the first?

SUGGESTED READINGS

Garber, E. D. *Cytogenetics: An Introduction.* New York: McGraw-Hill, 1972. See chap. 2.

Rhoades, M. M. "Meiosis," in J. Brachet and A. E. Mirsky (eds.), *The Cell*, vol. 3. New York: Academic, 1961, pp. 1–75.

Exercise 6

Sex Linkage

Sex linkage refers to traits which are transmitted on the X or the Y *chromosome*. Since the Y chromosome is small and carries few genes, most sex-linked traits are restricted to the X chromosome. Therefore, a female, with two X chromosomes, will carry a pair of alleles, while a male, with only one X chromosome, carries a single allele.

SAMPLE PROBLEM
A woman is a carrier for *color blindness*. Her husband is normal. What is the probability that her first son will be color-blind? What is the probability that any of her daughters will be color-blind?

ANSWER
Since the trait is inherited as a recessive, the mother's genotype is $X^C X^c$ and the father's is $X^C Y$. All sons will inherit the Y from the father. If they did not, they would not be sons. Note that the gene does not occur on the Y chromosome. Whether the son is color-blind depends entirely on whether he receives the X^C or the X^c from the mother. The probability of receiving the X^c, and therefore of being color-blind, is ½. All daughters, on the other hand, receive the X^C from the father. Since the C is dominant, all daughters will be normal, although the one-half receiving the X^c from the mother will be carriers.

56

PROBLEMS

1. *Hemophilia A* is inherited as an X-linked recessive. A woman has a brother with this defect. What is the probability that this woman will be a carrier if she herself is phenotypically normal?

2. Red-green color blindness is due to a recessive allele inherited on the X chromosome. In the following matings, give the probability that the son will have the defect:

    a. Carrier female × normal male
    b. Carrier female × color-blind male
    c. Color-blind female × normal male
    d. Homozygous dominant female × color-blind male

Could any of the above matings produce a color-blind daughter?

3. The *Xg blood-type system* is inherited on the X chromosome. The antigen is Xg and distinguishes two phenotypes, Xg-positive (Xg^+) and Xg-negative (Xg^-). The antigen is inherited as a dominant, although the phenotype of the heterozygous individual (female) is variable. A man who is Xg positive mates with a woman who is Xg negative. Give the possible blood types of sons and daughters and the probabilities.

4. A form of *defective tooth enamel* which leads to brown teeth appears to be inherited as an X-linked dominant. What is the probability that a son and daughter will have the trait in the following cases?

    a. Normal female × affected male
    b. Affected female (heterozygous) × normal male
    c. Affected female (homozygous) × normal male
    d. Affected female (heterozygous) × affected male

Exercise 6

ANSWERS AND DISCUSSION

1. If the woman's brother has the defect, his genotype must be $X^h Y$. Assuming his mother and father are phenotypically normal, their genotypes must be $X^H X^h$ and $X^H Y$, respectively. The woman received the X^H chromosome from her father. The probability of receiving the X^h from her mother, and thereby being a carrier, would be ½.

2. In this problem, the son always receives the Y from the father. The condition of the son is determined by the genotype of the mother. The important question is, what is the probability that the son will receive the X^c from the mother? The genotypes of the parents are given first:

   a. $X^C X^c \times X^C Y$; probability of receiving X^c from mother, ½
   b. $X^C X^c \times X^c Y$; probability of receiving X^c from mother, ½
   c. $X^c X^c \times X^C Y$; probability of receiving X^c from mother, 1
   d. $X^C X^C \times X^c Y$; probability of receiving X^c from mother, 0

A color-blind daughter must receive an X^c from both parents. This is possible only in problem *b*. Here the probability of receiving the X^c from the father is 1 and from the mother is ½. The probability of the daughter's being color-blind is therefore ½.

3. The genotypes are $X^- X^- \times X^+ Y$. All the sons have the genotype $X^- Y$ and are Xg^-, while all the daughters have the genotype $X^+ X^-$ and are Xg^+.

4. Again, as in problem 2, it is the genotype of the mother which determines the phenotype of the son, while the daughter's phenotype is determined by the genotypes of both parents. Remember, in this problem the trait is inherited as a dominant.

   a. $X^e X^e \times X^E Y$; all sons will be $X^e Y$ (normal) and all daughters $X^E X^e$ (affected).
   b. $X^E X^e \times X^e Y$; the probability is that ½ of the sons will be $X^E Y$ (affected) and ½ $X^e Y$ (normal), while ½ of the daughters will be $X^E X^e$ (affected) and ½ $X^e X^e$ (normal).
   c. $X^E X^E \times X^e Y$; all sons will be $X^E Y$ (affected) and all daughters $X^E X^e$ (affected).
   d. $X^E X^e \times X^E Y$; the probability is that ½ of the sons will be $X^E Y$ (affected) and ½ $X^e Y$ (normal), while ½ of the daughters will be $X^E X^E$ and ½ $X^E X^e$ (all affected).

PROBLEMS

Sex linkage can usually be identified in a pedigree. The following are three pedigrees involving sex linkage. Determine whether the trait is inherited as an X-linked dominant or an X-linked recessive and give the probable genotypes of the persons indicated.

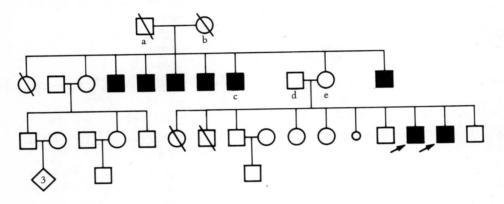

Figure 6-1a   Pedigree A.

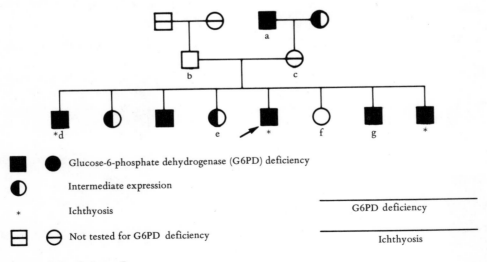

■ ● Glucose-6-phosphate dehydrogenase (G6PD) deficiency

◐ Intermediate expression

* Ichthyosis

⊟ ⊖ Not tested for G6PD deficiency

G6PD deficiency

Ichthyosis

Figure 6-1b   Pedigree B.

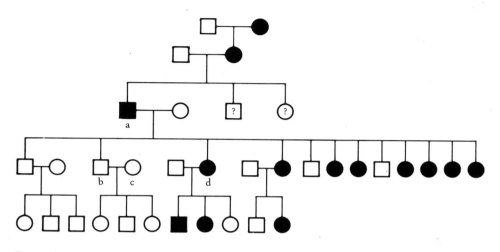

Figure 6-1c Pedigree C.

A. X-linked recessive. (a) $X^D Y$, (b) $X^D X^d$, (c) $X^d Y$, (d) $X^D Y$, (e) $X^D X^d$.

B. X-linked recessives. (a) $X^g Y \, X^I Y$, (b) $X^G Y \, X^I Y$, (c) $X^G X^g \, X^I X^i$, (d) $X^g Y \, X^i Y$, (e) $X^G X^g \, X^I X^I$ or $X^I X^i$, (f) $X^G X^G \, X^I X^I$ or $X^I X^i$, (g) $X^g Y \, X^I Y$.

C. X-linked dominant. (a) $X^B Y$, (b) $X^b Y$, (c) $X^b X^b$, (d) $X^B X^b$.

These pedigrees are actual published pedigrees of (A) congenital deafness, (B) glucose-6-phosphate dehydrogenase (G6PD) deficiency and X-linked ichthyosis, and (C) brown tooth enamel. These abnormalities are defined in the glossary. The pedigrees were published in the following articles:

A. K. N. McRae et al., "Sex-Linked Congenital Deafness," *American Journal of Human Genetics,* 21 (1969), 416.

B. G. Filippi and P. Meera Khan, "Linkage Studies on X-Linked Ichthyosis in Sardinia," *American Journal of Human Genetics,* 21 (1968), 566.

C. J. B. S. Haldane, "A Probable New Sex-Linked Dominant in Man," *Journal of Heredity,* 28 (1937), 59.

SUGGESTED READINGS
McKusick, V. A. "On the X Chromosome of Man," *Quarterly Review of Biology,* 37 (1962), 69–175.

McKusick, V. A. *Human Genetics.* 2d ed. Englewood Cliffs, N.J.: Prentice-Hall, 1969. See chaps. 2 and 3.

Winchester, A. M. *Human Genetics.* Columbus: Merrill, 1971. See chaps. 5 and 6.

Exercise 7

Blood Typing

Human populations are *polymorphic;* that is, within human populations many traits occur in two or more variants, each occurring in more than 1 percent of the individuals. One example of this polymorphism is hair color. In an American classroom we find various shades of black, brown, red, and blond hair colors. Such polymorphism is also found among blood proteins. A *blood-type system* is a set of proteins controlled by a single gene or closely linked set of genes. The best-known system is the *ABO blood-type system.* There are two genetically determined proteins in this system called *antigens* A and B. An individual's blood may contain the A or B, both, or neither, thus giving rise to the four ABO blood types A, B, AB, and O.

   Antibodies can be used to detect the presence of proteins in the blood and thus type the individual. When one of the ABO system antibodies is added to a sample of blood, it either will not react at all with the sample or will cause the clumping or *agglutination* of the red cells in the sample. Thus anti-A antibodies will detect the presence of antigen A by agglutinating the sample and anti-B will detect the presence of antigen B. The blood of an AB individual will have an agglutination response to both antibodies, while the blood of an O individual will respond to neither.

PROBLEMS
1. Before actually typing a blood sample, we should be clear on how to read the results of the test. In the table below, the various blood types are listed. Fill in with a + for agglutination or a − for no agglutination in the appropriate column.

Blood Type	Anti-A	Anti-B
A		
B		
AB		
O		

2. In order to carry out the blood-typing procedure, you need two drops of whole blood. This can be an unknown sample provided for you, or you can type your own blood. Follow these instructions carefully if you are going to use your own blood:

   a. Have the following materials in front of you before you start: alcohol, cotton, gauze, unwrapped sterile blood lancet, a clean microscopic slide marked A at one end and B at the other with grease pencil, toothpicks, and the bottles of antiserum.

   b. Wash your hands and swab alcohol over the fingertip from which you plan to draw blood. Let the alcohol evaporate. Be careful not to contaminate the finger while preparing for the next step.

   c. Take the unused blood lancet and prick the finger. Throw the lancet away. Never use a blood lancet over again.

   d. Squeeze out a drop of blood and wipe it off your finger with a sterile gauze pad saturated with alcohol. This first drop may contain few blood cells. Then place a drop of blood at each end of the slide. Cover the "wound" with the gauze.

   e. Place a drop of anti-A on one drop of blood and a drop of anti-B on the other. Be sure that the tip of the dropper never touches the blood sample. Take a clean toothpick and mix the blood and antisera together. Use different toothpicks or opposite ends of the same toothpick for each sample.

   f. Observe the presence or absence of agglutination in each sample. Sometimes a gentle rocking back and forth of the slide will permit easier observation of the reaction. The observation should be made within three minutes, before coagulation takes place or the blood plus antiserum dries.

Using the table which you have prepared, determine your blood type or the type of the sample given you, and record this on the chart on page 63. Also record the blood types of other members of your class.

3. Other antibodies can be used to determine the presence or absence of other blood proteins. For example, we can test for the *Rh system*. This blood-type system is extremely complex, and many proteins are involved. However, in the United States the one usually tested for is RH_0. In this population approximately 14 percent lack this protein and are therefore Rh_0^-.

To determine Rh blood type, follow the directions for the ABO determination, but use only one drop of blood. Place one drop of the anti-Rh_0 on the drop of blood. Mix and then wait a few minutes, but not more than three, before reading. In this particular case the clumps of red cells are small and are sometimes difficult to see; so you might want to use a magnifying glass. Record your blood type and those of other class members on the chart.

4. Another blood-type system which is easy to determine is the MN. Here we are dealing with two proteins, M and N. Since they are determined by two codominant alleles, we have only three possible blood types: M, N, and MN. Following the same instructions as in problem 2, determine your MN blood type and record the appropriate data on the chart.

5. When you have finished typing your own blood, collect the data on blood types of other members of your class. Calculate the percentages of the varying ABO, Rh, and MN blood types of your class.

6. One study of 141,774 blood donors gives the following distribution of ABO blood types in the United States: 45.6 percent O, 40.8 percent A, 10.0 percent B, and 3.7 percent AB.[1] Compare the ABO frequencies of your class to these percentages. There are a number of factors which could explain the differences between your class frequencies and the national frequencies, including small sample size and differences in ethnic mixture.

SUGGESTED READINGS

Race, R. R., and R. Sanger. *Blood Groups in Man.* 5th ed. Oxford: Blackwell Scientific, 1968.

Snyder, L. H. *Blood Groups.* Minneapolis: Burgess, 1973.

[1]G. W. Hervey, L. K. Diamond, and V. Watson, "Geographic Blood Group Variability in the United States," *Journal of the American Medical Association,* 145 (1951), 80–81.

Name _____ Class _____ Date _____

Blood-Type Systems

Record your blood types here:

ABO system   _____

Rh system   _____

MN system   _____

Record data for your class below:

ABO system	Number	Percent
Type A	_____	_____
Type B	_____	_____
Type AB	_____	_____
Type O	_____	_____

Rh system		
Type $RH_o{}^+$	_____	_____
Type $RH_o{}^-$	_____	_____

MN system		
Type M	_____	_____
Type N	_____	_____
Type MN	_____	_____

Be sure to save this page for use in Exercise 9.

Exercise 8

Blood Problems

A great deal of work has been done on the determination of blood types in various populations as a measure of human variability. Unlike many traits, blood types are easy to determine and quantify; they are not affected by the environment; and the mechanisms of inheritance for many blood-type systems are precisely known. This exercise deals with a series of genetic problems involving the ABO, Rh, and MN blood-type systems.

The blood types in the ABO system are determined by three alleles. By convention, one letter is used to indicate one *gene,* and alternate forms of that letter are used to indicate the various *alleles.* The letter I will be used here for the ABO gene. There are two *codominant* alleles, I^A and I^B, which are responsible for the production of the *antigens* A and B, respectively. The recessive, i, results in no antigen production. Therefore a person with genotype ii would be blood type O, whereas persons with either $I^A I^A$ or $I^A i$ would be blood type A. A person with $I^B I^B$ or $I^B i$ would be blood type B. A person with both dominant alleles $I^A I^B$ would be blood type AB. RH^+ is inherited as a simple dominant. MN blood types are determined by two codominant alleles, L^M and L^N.

PROBLEMS

1. Given the following matings and the blood types of the parents, what would the blood types of the offspring be? Give all possibilities and their probabilities:

    a. O × O
    b. O × A (homozygous)
    c. O × A (heterozygous)
    d. O × AB
    e. A × B (both heterozygous)
    f. AB × AB

2. A man of blood type AB mates with a woman who is heterozygous for blood type B. Give the possible blood types of the offspring and the probabilities for each.

3. In a recent court case, a man of blood type A was accused of fathering a child of blood type B. The mother was blood type AB. Could this man have been the father?

4. A woman is blood type A, Rh-positive (heterozygous for both), and her mate is O, Rh-positive (heterozygous). Give the possible blood types of their offspring and the probabilities for each.

5. A man who is type MN mates with a woman who is type N. Give the possible blood types of their offspring and the probabilities for each.

Exercise 8

6. For the following mating give the possible blood types of the offspring and the probabilities for each: O, Rh-positive (heterozygous), M × AB, Rh-negative, MN.

ANSWERS

1. The left column gives the genotypes of the parents. The right column gives the genotype and phenotype of the offspring.

a.	$ii \times ii$	all ii (O)
b.	$ii \times I^A I^A$	all $I^A i$ (A)
c.	$ii \times I^A i$	½ $I^A i$ (A), ½ ii (O)
d.	$ii \times I^A I^B$	½ $I^A i$ (A), ½ $I^B i$ (B)
e.	$I^A i \times I^B i$	¼ $I^A i$ (A), ¼ $I^A I^B$ (AB), ¼ $I^B i$ (B), ¼ ii (O)
f.	$I^A I^B \times I^A I^B$	¼ $I^A I^A$ (A), ½ $I^A I^B$ (AB), ¼ $I^B I^B$ (B)

2. $I^A I^B \times I^B i$ ¼ $I^A I^B$ (AB), ¼ $I^B I^B$ + ¼ $I^B i$ (½ B), ¼ $I^A i$ (A)

3. Yes. The child's genotype is either $I^B I^B$ or $I^B i$ and the mother's is $I^A I^B$. The child could have received an I^B from the mother and an i from the father. This child could have been fathered by the following types: A ($I^A i$), B ($I^B I^B$, $I^B i$), AB ($I^A I^B$), or O (ii).

4. The genotypes of the parents are $I^A i Rhrh$ and $ii Rhrh$: This is a problem in independent assortment. Therefore, we can separate the problem into two distinct problems: (a) $I^A i \times ii$ and (b) $Rhrh \times Rhrh$. The answer to the first problem is ½ $I^A i$ (A) and ½ ii (O), and the answer to the second problem is ¼ $RhRh$ + ½ $Rhrh$ (¾ RH+) and ¼ $rhrh$ (¼ Rh−). We then have four possible combinations, as follows: A Rh+ (½ × ¾ = ⅜), A Rh− (½ × ¼ = ⅛), O Rh+ (½ × ¾ = ⅜), and O Rh− (½ × ¼ = ⅛).

5. The genotypes of the parents are $L^M L^N$ and $L^N L^N$. The two possible combinations are ½ $L^M L^N$ (MN) and ½ $L^N L^N$ (N).

6. This is another problem in independent assortment. The mating can be written: $ii Rhrh L^M L^M \times I^A I^B rhrh L^M L^N$. This can be broken down into three separate problems, as follows: (a) $ii \times I^A I^B$ = ½ $I^A i$ (A), ½ $I^B i$ (B), (b) $Rhrh \times rhrh$ = ½ $Rhrh$ (Rh$^+$), ½ $rhrh$ (½ Rh−), (c) $L^M L^M \times L^M L^N$ = ½ $L^M L^M$ (M), ½ $L^M L^N$ (MN). We have eight possible combinations: A Rh+ M, A Rh+ MN, A Rh− M, A Rh− MN, B Rh+ M, B Rh+ MN, B Rh− M, and B Rh− MN. The probability of each is ½ × ½ × ½ = ⅛.

Exercise 9

Using the Hardy-Weinberg Formula

In genetic terms, a *population* can be said to be evolving if there are changes in the frequencies of alleles within that population's *gene pool.* Conversely, the lack of such changes indicates a state in which the population is not *evolving.* Such a state is termed *genetic equilibrium.* Genetic equilibrium would be possible only under the conditions of infinite population size, random mating, equal fertility for all matings, and no mutations. Since no population meets these conditions, the state of genetic equilibrium is a hypothetical situation useful for certain mathematical calculations involving the effect of evolutionary forces on populations.

Genetic equilibrium can be defined in terms of a mathematical model, known as the *Hardy-Weinberg formula: $p^2 + 2pq + q^2 = 1$.* In this formula p stands for the frequency of the allele A, and q stands for the frequency of the allele a. This can be written as follows, with the brackets standing for "frequency of": $[A] = p$ and $[a] = q$. Since the gene in question has only two alleles, the sum of their frequencies must equal 1, or totality. Thus, $p + q = 1$.

If $[A] = p$, $[AA] = p^2$. If $[a] = q$, $[aa] = q^2$. It also follows that $[Aa] = 2pq$. Since these are the only genotypes possible, their frequencies must equal 1. Thus, $p^2 + 2pq + q^2 = 1$.

The assumption that genetic equilibrium exists allows us to calculate what allele frequencies would exist for a particular gene if no evolutionary forces were working. The way in which the real situation deviates from the ideal gives a measure of the amount of evolutionary change that has occurred. Then the formula can be used to answer a number of significant questions. Problems using the Hardy-Weinberg formula can be rather complex. However, since our purpose here is to introduce the beginning student to the general types of problems which can be worked, we shall present relatively uncomplicated types of problems.

68

CALCULATING ALLELE FREQUENCIES

The Hardy-Weinberg formula can be used to calculate the frequencies of the various alleles in a population, assuming genetic equilibrium. For example, a survey was made on a large college campus to determine what proportion of the student population can roll their tongues (see Exercise 1). In this survey it was determined that out of 1,000 college students, 160 could not accomplish this act. What are the frequencies of the alleles R and r?

We are given the frequency of the homozygous recessive genotype, the only genotype which results in the inability to roll one's tongue. Thus, $[rr] = q^2 = 0.16$. The figure 0.16 is derived from the data, 160/1,000, or 16 percent. To determine the frequency of r we simply take the square root of 0.16. Thus, $[r] = q = \sqrt{0.16} = 0.4$. To find $[p]$, we use the following formula: $p + q = 1$. From this, it follows that $[R] = p = 1 - q = 1 - 0.4 = 0.6$. The frequencies of R and r are 0.6 and 0.4 respectively, or, to put it another way, R comprises 60 percent and r 40 percent of the gene pool.

In many ways it is easier to calculate the allele frequencies for X-linked traits. If, in a given population, 1 percent of the males are color-blind, we would calculate the allele frequencies as follows: $[X^c] = q = 0.01$. Note that the frequency of the allele X^c is the same as the frequency of the genotype $X^c Y$, since the c is not found on the Y chromosome. From this it follows that $[X^C] = p = 1 - q = 1 - 0.01 = 0.99$.

PROBLEMS

1. In a given population, 36 percent had attached earlobes (which results from a homozygous recessive genotype), while the rest had free-hanging earlobes. Calculate the frequencies of the two alleles, E and e.

2. Look up your class data from Exercise 1. Calculate the allele frequencies for the traits listed. Since you probably will not be taking simple square roots, you will need to use a calculator or locate a table of square roots.

Using the Hardy-Weinberg Formula

3. In a given population, 4 percent were homozygous for sickle-cell anemia. Calculate the frequency of the alleles involved.

4. In a given population, 3 percent of the males had glucose-6-phosphate-dehydrogenase (G6PD) deficiency. This trait results from the inheritance of a recessive allele on the X chromosome. Calculate the allele frequencies.

ANSWERS

1. $[ee] = q^2 = 0.36$
$[e] = q = \sqrt{0.36} = 0.6$
$[E] = p = 1 - q = 1 - 0.6$
$\quad = 0.4$

2. (Frequencies will depend on class data)

3. $[Hb^S Hb^S] = q^2 = 0.04$
$[Hb^S] = q = \sqrt{0.04} = 0.2$
$[Hb^A] = p = 1 - q = 1 - 0.2 = 0.8$

4. $[X^g] = q = 0.03$
$[X^G] = p = 1 - q = 1 - 0.03$
$\quad = 0.97$

CALCULATING GENOTYPIC FREQUENCIES
After the allele frequencies have been determined, as in the problems above, it is possible to calculate the frequencies of the various genotypes.

For example, in the example under "Calculating Allele Frequencies" for tongue rolling, $[A] = p = 0.6$ and $[a] = q = 0.4$. The genotypes can be determined as follows: $[AA] = p^2 = (0.6)^2 = 0.36$; $[Aa] = 2pq = 2 \times 0.6 \times 0.4 = 0.48$; $[aa] = q^2 = (0.4)^2 = 0.16$.

PROBLEMS
1. Using the results of problem 1, page 69, calculate the frequencies of the three genotypes.

2. Using the results of problem 2, page 69, calculate the frequencies of the various genotypes.

3. Using the results of problem 3, page 70, calculate the frequencies of the three phenotypes: "normal," sickle-cell trait (heterozygous), and sickle-cell anemia.

4. Using the results of problem 4, page 70, calculate the frequencies of the three genotypes among females. What percentage of females have G6PD deficiency? Why is this so much lower than the percentage of males with the abnormality?

ANSWERS

1. $[EE] = p^2 = (0.4)^2 = 0.16$
$[Ee] = 2pq = 2(0.4)(0.6) = 0.48$
$[ee] - q^2 = (0.6)^2 = 0.36$

2. (Frequencies will depend on the class data)

3. $[Hb^A Hb^A] = p^2 = (0.8)^2 = 0.64$
$[Hb^A Hb^S] = 2pq = 2(0.8)(0.2) = 0.32$
$[Hb^S Hb^S] = q^2 = (0.2)^2 = 0.04$

4. $[X^G Y] = p = 0.97$
$[X^g Y] = q = 0.03$
$[X^G X^G] = p^2 = (0.97)^2 = 0.9409$
$[X^G X^g] = 2pq = 2(0.97)(0.03)$
$\qquad = 0.0582$
$[X^g X^g] = q^2 = (0.03)^2 = 0.0009$

DETERMINING THE STATE OF GENETIC EQUILIBRIUM

The Hardy-Weinberg formula can be used to determine whether a particular population is in genetic equilibrium.

For example, we can take a hypothetical population with the following genotypic frequencies: $[AA] = 0.34$, $[Aa] = 0.46$, and $[aa] = 0.20$. Is this population in genetic equilibrium with respect to the A gene?

To calculate the frequency of A, we add the frequency of the AA individuals, who contribute only A alleles to the gene pool, and one-half the frequency of the Aa individuals, since only one-half of their alleles are A. Therefore, $[A] = p = [AA] + \frac{1}{2}[Aa] = 0.34 + \frac{1}{2}(0.46) = 0.34 + 0.23 = 0.57$. Since $p = 0.57$, $q = 0.43$.

To determine if this population is in genetic equilibrium, we take the calculated allele frequencies and determine the expected frequencies of the genotypes: $[AA] = p^2 = (0.57)^2 = 0.325$; $[Aa] = 2pq = 2(0.57)(0.43) = 0.490$; $[aa] = q^2 = (0.43)^2 = 0.185$. When these figures are compared to the observed frequencies, it can be seen that they do not agree.[1] Therefore, our population is not in genetic equilibrium with respect to the gene.

PROBLEMS

1. In a given population the genotypic frequencies are $[BB] = 0.60$, $[Bb] = 0.30$, and $[bb] = 0.10$. Is this population in genetic equilibrium?

2. The following chart gives the phenotypic frequencies for the MN blood-type system in three populations. Calculate the expected frequencies of M, MN, and N blood types and determine in each case if the population is in genetic equilibrium with respect to this blood-type system.

Population	M(%)	MN(%)	N(%)
Navaho	84.5	14.4	1.1
Australian aborigine	2.4	30.4	67.2
English	28.7	47.4	23.9

Data from A. E. Mourant et al., *The Distribution of the Human Blood Groups and Other Polymorphisms*, 2d ed. (London: Oxford Univ. Press, 1976).

[1] The amount of disagreement between the expected and observed frequencies may or may not be significant. Statistical methods exist, which will not be discussed here, for evaluating the significance.

ANSWERS

1. $[B] = p = [BB] + \frac{1}{2}[Bb] = 0.60 + \frac{1}{2}(0.30) = 0.60 + 0.15 = 0.75$
   $[b] = q = 1 - 0.75 = 0.25$

	[BB]	[Bb]	[bb]
Exp. Freq.	0.5625	0.3750	0.0625
Obs. Freq.	0.6000	0.3000	0.1000

2.

Population	Exp. Freq.			Obs. Freq.				
	[M]	[MN]	[N]	[M]	[MN]	[N]	[L^M]	[L^N]
Navaho	0.841	0.152	0.007	0.845	0.144	0.011	0.917	0.083
Australian aborigine	0.031	0.290	0.679	0.024	0.304	0.672	0.176	0.824
English	0.275	0.499	0.227	0.287	0.474	0.239	0.524	0.476

PROBLEMS INVOLVING MULTIPLE ALLELES

The ABO blood-type system is determined by three alleles. In this situation $[I^A] = p$, $[I^B] = q$, and $[i] = r$, and $p + q + r = 1$. Therefore, $p^2 + 2pq + 2pr + q^2 + 2qr + r^2 = 1$.

As an example, we can take the following allelic frequencies: $[I^A] = 0.2$, $[I^B] = 0.1$, and $[i] = 0.7$. Calculate the frequencies of blood types A, B, AB, and O.

The frequencies of the four blood types are determined as follows:

$[A] = [I^A I^A] + [I^A i] = p^2 + 2pr = (0.2)^2 + 2(0.2)(0.7) = 0.04 + 0.28 = 0.32$

$[B] = [I^B I^B] + [I^B i] = q^2 + 2qr = (0.1)^2 + 2(0.1)(0.7) = 0.01 + 0.14 = 0.15$

$[AB] = [I^A I^B] = 2pq = 2(0.2)(0.1) = 0.04$

$[O] = [ii] = r^2 = (0.7)^2 = 0.49$

It is also possible to calculate allele frequencies from population data. For example, in one study in London, England, the frequencies of blood types O, A, B, and AB were 0.546, 0.356, 0.088, and 0.010, respectively.[2] There is a fairly simple method whereby the frequencies of the alleles I^A, I^B, and i can be estimated. The three formulas used are

$$r = \sqrt{[O]} \qquad p = \sqrt{[A] + [O]} - r \qquad q = 1 - (p + r)$$

[2]A. E. Mourant et al., *The Distribution of the Human Blood Groups and Other Polymorphisms*, 2d ed. (London: Oxford Univ. Press, 1976).

Using the data given above for London, we can estimate the allele frequencies as follows:

$$r = \sqrt{0.546} = 0.739$$

$$p = \sqrt{0.356 + 0.546} - 0.739 = 0.211$$

$$q = 1 - (0.739 + 0.211) = 0.050$$

PROBLEMS

1. In a given population the frequency of allele I^A is 0.3 and that of I^B is 0.2. Calculate the frequencies of the blood types A, B, AB, and O.

2. The following table gives the ABO blood-type frequencies for three populations. Using these data, calculate the frequencies of I^A, I^B, and i for each population.

	Frequency of			
Population	O	A	B	AB
Gorkha, Nepal	0.318	0.338	0.252	0.092
Cherokee Indian, U.S.A.	0.956	0.037	0.007	0.000
Yoruba, Nigeria	0.523	0.215	0.231	0.031

Data from A. E. Mourant et al., *The Distribution of the Human Blood Groups and Other Polymorphisms*, 2d ed. (London: Oxford Univ. Press, 1976).

3. Using the data from Exercise 7, calculate the allele frequencies for your class.

ANSWERS

1. $[I^A] = p = 0.3$

   $[I^B] = q = 0.2$

   $[i] = r = 1 - p - q = 1 - 0.3 - 0.2 = 0.5$

   $[A] = [I^AI^A] + [I^Ai] = p^2 + 2pr = (0.3)^2 + 2(0.3)(0.5) = 0.09 + 0.30 = 0.39$

   $[B] = [I^BI^B] + [I^Bi] = q^2 + 2qr = (0.2)^2 + 2(0.2)(0.5) = 0.04 + 0.20 = 0.24$

   $[AB] = [I^AI^B] = 2pq = 2(0.3)(0.2) = 0.12$

   $[O] = [ii] = r^2 = (0.5)^2 = 0.25$

2.

Population	p	q	r
Nepal	0.246	0.190	0.564
Cherokee	0.018	0.004	0.978
Yoruba	0.136	0.141	0.723

3. (Frequencies will depend on class data.)

SUGGESTED READINGS

Baldwin, R. E. *Genetics.* New York: Wiley, 1973. See chap. 6.

Bodmer, W. F., and L. L. Cavalli-Sforza. *Genetics, Evolution, and Man.* San Francisco: Freeman, 1976. See chap. 6.

Cavalli-Sforza, L. L., and W. F. Bodmer. *The Genetics of Human Populations.* San Francisco: Freeman, 1971.

Mettler, L. E., and T. C. Gregg. *Population Genetics and Evolution.* Englewood Cliffs, N.J.: Prentice-Hall, 1969.

Morris, L. N. *Human Populations, Genetic Variation, and Evolution.* San Francisco: Chandler, 1971. See chap. 1.

Wallace, B. *Population Genetics.* Boston: Heath, 1964.

Exercise 10

Sampling Error

Sampling error results from small population size. One of the requirements for genetic equilibrium is an infinite population size. Since this condition is never met, gene frequencies will change on the basis of chance. This type of fluctuation in gene frequency, called *genetic drift*, is most pronounced in very small populations.

To illustrate sampling error, flip a coin 10 times and record the number of heads on Chart A. Repeat until you have 10 trials of 10 recorded. Next, record your data on Graph A. Indicate the number of times you flipped 5 heads, 4 heads, etc., during your 10 trials. Since the probability of landing heads is ½, you would expect to land 5 heads each time. How often did you land 5 heads? What conclusion can you draw from looking at the graph?

Returning to Chart A, record the deviation from the expected for each trial. The expected is 5. If you recorded 4 heads, then your deviation for that trial is 1. To obtain the percent deviation, we ask the question, what percent of 5 is 1? The answer is 20 percent. Calculate the percent deviation for each trial.

Now total up your 10 trials to obtain a sample of 100 flips of the coin. You would expect to obtain 50 heads in this sample. Calculate your deviation and percent deviation from this expectation.

Then, using data from your classmates, add 4 other series to yours to obtain a sample of 500 flips. Add more until you get 1,000 or more. Enter these data on Chart B. What happens to the percent deviation as the size of the sample becomes greater? Show this on Graph B.

SUGGESTED READINGS

Bodmer, W. F., and L. L. Cavalli-Sforza. *Genetics, Evolution, and Man.* San Francisco: Freeman, 1976. See chap. 12.

Morris, L. N. (ed.). *Human Populations, Genetic Variation, and Evolution.* San Francisco: Chandler, 1971. See chap. 5.

Exercise 12

Biostatistics

Natural selection is the process that leads to a different survival rate for the possessors of different genotypes. In other words, natural selection refers to differential mortality and fertility rates. In order to analyze natural selection, it becomes necessary to compute these rates. This exercise deals with some of the basic methods for making such determinations.

MORTALITY

There are several measures of *mortality;* the type used depends on the nature of the study. The simplest is the *crude death rate,* given by the formula $m = \frac{D}{P} k$. In this formula m is the crude death rate, D is the total number of deaths in a specific population during a calendar year (January 1 through December 31); P is the average size of the population, usually on July 1 of that year; and k is a constant, usually 1,000 or 100,000, depending on how one wishes to express the crude death rate (e.g., in terms of deaths per 1,000 or deaths per 100,000 individuals).

Example In a given population of 300,000 individuals in 1880, 65 persons died. Calculate the crude death rate.

In this situation $D = 65$, $P = 300,000$, and we will assume that $k = 100,000$. The crude death rate is calculated as follows:

$$m = \frac{D}{P} k = \frac{65}{300,000} \times 100,000 = 21.7$$

The crude death rate is 21.7 per 100,000.

It is possible to calculate a crude death rate for a specific cause, such as cancer or automobile accidents. The formula used is the same one used for the crude death rate, although it is written as $m^i = \dfrac{D^i}{P} = k$, where m^i refers to the crude death rate for a specific cause and D^i refers to the number of deaths during a calendar year due to that specific cause.

Example In a given population of 150,000, 10 persons died of cancer in 1970. Calculate the crude death rate for cancer.

In this problem $D^i = 10, P = 150,000$, and we will assume that $k = 1,000$. The specific death rate is calculated as follows:

$$m^i = \frac{D^i}{P}k = \frac{10}{150,000} \times 1,000 = 0.067 \text{ per } 1,000$$

This is the same as 6.7 per 100,000 if we choose $k = 100,000$.

Often a researcher wishes to calculate death rates for various segments of the population, such as sex and age categories or ethnic groups. For this purpose we can determine a *specific death rate*. Again, the formula is identical to the ones above, except that D and P refer to specific categories of individuals.

Example In a given population of 200,000 individuals there are 90,000 males. In 1948, 14 of these males died. Assume $k = 100,000$. Calculate the specific death rate for males.

In this problem $D^i = 14, P = 90,000$, and $k = 100,000$. We can calculate the death rate for this group as follows:

$$m^i = \frac{D^i}{P}k = \frac{14}{90,000} \times 100,000 = 15.6 \text{ per } 100,000$$

INFANT MORTALITY

Infant mortality can be measured by the *crude infant death rate*, which is computed by use of the following formula: $q = \dfrac{D_0^z}{B^z} k$. In this formula q refers to the crude infant death rate, D_0^z to the number of deaths between birth and age one year for a given community during year z, B^z to the total number of live births within year z, and k to the constant (1,000 or 100,000). This is the basic infant mortality rate formula. However, since some deaths in year z will occur for babies born in the preceding year and some babies born in year z will die in the following year before they reach the age of one year, more complicated forms of the above must be used to determine infant mortality accurately.

Example In a population in which there were 100,000 births in 1953, 6,000 infants between birth and one year of age died. Calculate the crude infant death rate. Assume $k = 1,000$.

Exercise 12

In this problem $D_0^z = 6,000$, $B^z = 100,000$, and $k = 1,000$. The crude infant death rate is determined as follows:

$$q = \frac{D_0^z}{B^z} k = \frac{6,000}{100,000} \times 1,000 = 60 \text{ per } 1,000$$

FERTILITY

As with mortality, there are several measures of *fertility*. However, one general formula can be used: $i = \frac{B}{P} k$. In this formula, i is the *crude birth rate*, B is the total number of live births during a calendar year among members of a specific community, and P is the average number of persons living in that community during that year. The constant k is usually set at 1,000.

The crude birth rate takes all persons in the community into account, including all males, children, and the elderly. More precise measures of fertility are called *general fertility rates*. Of these, the most useful is one in which the above formula is used but P is taken to be the total female population of reproductive age, usually between the ages of fifteen and forty-four.

The formula can also be used to determine *specific fertility rates*. These are fertility rates for specific segments of the population, such as a particular ethnic group or socioeconomic class. In these cases B equals the total number of births for the segment in question and P the total number of women of reproductive age for this same segment.

Example In a given population in a given year there were 3,000 births. The population contains 50,000 women between the ages of fifteen and forty-four. Calculate the general fertility rate.

To calculate the general fertility rate we use the formula as follows:

$$i = \frac{B}{P} k = \frac{3,000}{50,000} \times 1,000 = 60 \text{ per } 1,000$$

PROBLEMS

In the following problems you will be asked to derive mortality and fertility rates from actual data. The answers will be found at the end of this exericse.

1. In 1968 the United States population was about 203,000,000. The number of deaths in that year was 1,950,000. What was the crude death rate? ($k = 1,000$)

2. In 1968 the population of Turkey was about 34,400,000, and the number of deaths in that year was about 620,000. What was the crude death rate? ($k = 1,000$)

3. In 1940 the crude death rate in Ceylon was 2,140 per 100,000. In that year the population was about 6,000,000 and about 7,400 people died of malaria. What was the crude death rate for malaria? ($k = 100,000$)

4. Calculate the specific death rate for the age category fifteen to twenty-four on the basis of the following data from England in 1933: of 6,600,000 people between the ages of fifteen and twenty-four, 18,200 died. ($k = 1,000$)

5. In 1948 in Japan there were 1,378,564 live births. Of these, 90,779 babies died before the first year of life. What is the crude infant death rate? ($k = 1,000$)

6. In 1968 there were 3,540,000 live births in the United States. The population was about 203,000,000 in that year. What is the crude birth rate? ($k = 1,000$)

7. In problem 6, the total female population between the ages of fifteen and forty-four was about 41,500,000. What was the general fertility rate? ($k = 1,000$)

8. The 1968 crude birth rate was at a record low. Some people have taken this as a general indication of a change in United States birth practices in the direction of zero population growth. However, the general fertility rate is not at an all-time low (it was lower in the mid-1930s during the Depression). Explain the discrepancy between the two indications of fertility.

ANSWERS

1. $m = \dfrac{D}{P} k$

$$m = \dfrac{1,950,000}{203,000,000} \times 1,000$$

$m = 9.6$ per 1,000

2. $m = \dfrac{D}{P} k$

$$m = \dfrac{620,000}{34,400,000} \times 1,000$$

$m = 18$ per 1,000

3. $m^i = \dfrac{D^i}{P} k$

$$m^i = \dfrac{7,400}{6,000,000} \times 100,000$$

$m^i = 123$ per 100,000 (This death rate dropped to 13 per 100,000 in 1951 after DDT had been used for five years.)

4. $m^i = \dfrac{D^i}{P} k$

$$m^i = \dfrac{18,200}{6,600,000} \times 1,000$$

$m^i = 2.8$ per 1,000

5. $q = \dfrac{D^{\tilde{z}}_{\tilde{0}}}{B^z} k$

$$q = \dfrac{90,779}{1,378,564} \times 1,000$$

$q = 65.9$ per 1,000

6. $i = \dfrac{B}{P} k$

$$i = \dfrac{3,540,000}{203,000,000} \times 1,000$$

$i = 17.4$ per 1,000

7.
$$i = \frac{B}{P} k \quad \text{\footnotesize females between fifteen and forty-four}$$

$$i = \frac{3{,}540{,}000}{41{,}500{,}000} \times 1{,}000$$

$$i = 85.3 \text{ per } 1{,}000$$

8. The crude birth rate is low because the proportion of women of reproductive age in the late 1960s was lower than in preceding years. The general fertility rate is based only on these women.

SUGGESTED READINGS

Barclay, G. W. *Techniques of Populaton Analysis*. New York: Wiley, 1958.

Chiang, C. L. *Biostatistics*. New York: Krieger, 1975.

Sokal, R. R. and J. Rohlf. *Introduction to Biostatistics*. San Francisco: Freeman, 1973.

Spiegelman, M. *Introduction to Demography*. Cambridge: Harvard Univ. Press, 1968.

Exercise 13

Natural Selection

The concept of *natural selection* was summed up by Charles Darwin in the Introduction to *The Origin of Species:*

As many more individuals of each species are born than can possibly survive; and as, consequently, there is a frequently recurring struggle for existence, it follows that any being, if it vary however slightly in any manner profitable to itself, under the complex and sometimes varying conditions of life, will have a better chance of surviving, and thus be naturally selected. From the strong principle of inheritance, any selected variety will tend to propagate its new and modified form. [1]

The modern concept of natural selection is based upon the observation that all populations display genetic variability and that these genetic variants will show differences in fertility and mortality, thereby making differing contributions to the next generation. Using a very simple, artificial situation, this exercise illustrates how color and size might operate in a specific situation as factors upon which natural selection might work.

For this exercise you will need three sheets of white and three sheets of black construction paper, 8½ by 11 inches. Keep one sheet of each color for backgrounds. Cut the other sheets into squares to obtain the following:

16 one-inch squares, white	16 one-inch squares, black
10 half-inch squares, white	6 half-inch squares, black
10 quarter-inch squares, white	6 quarter-inch squares, black

[1] Darwin, *The Origin of Species* (New York: Modern Library), p. 13.

Selection for Color Take 16 of each color of the one-inch squares and spread them out as randomly as possible on a piece of black paper. Have a person who is unaware of the significance of this exercise pick out 16 of the 32 squares as rapidly as possible (within ten seconds). On the sheet provided, record the number of black and white squares selected. Repeat with the same 32 squares on a white background. Repeat the procedure with at least four persons or collect data from four others doing the same exercise.

Selection for Size Take 10 each of the one-inch, half-inch, and quarter-inch white squares and spread them out on the white background. Have a friend pick out 15 squares as rapidly as possible and record on the data sheet the numbers of each size chosen. Repeat with at least five people acting as the "selective agent."

Selection for Color and Size Take 6 each of the one-inch, half-inch, and quarter-inch white and black squares for a total of 36 squares. Mix them thoroughly and spread them out on a black background. Have at least five people pick up 18 of these squares as rapidly as possible. Record the squares chosen.

PROBLEMS

1. Calculate the expected results for each of the parts as if the choosing process were totally random. Record your data on the appropriate answer sheet. How do the squares actually chosen compare to the expected number? Was the choosing actually random?

2. What factors were responsible for the results actually obtained?

SUGGESTED READINGS

Bajema, C. J. (ed.). *Natural Selection in Human Populations.* New York: Wiley, 1971.

Bodmer, W. F., and L. L. Cavalli-Sforza. *Genetics, Evolution, and Man.* San Francisco: Freeman, 1976. See chap. 7.

Sheppard, P. M. *Natural Selection and Heredity.* New York: Harper & Row, 1959.

Volpe, E. P. *Understanding Evolution,* 2nd ed. Dubuque, Iowa: Wm. C. Brown, 1971.

Name _____ Class _____ Date _____

1. Selection for Color

Trial	No. Black Squares		Percent Deviation from Expected*	Background Color
	Expected	Selected		
1	_____	_____	_____	Black
2	_____	_____	_____	Black
3	_____	_____	_____	Black
4	_____	_____	_____	Black
5	_____	_____	_____	Black
Total	_____	_____	_____	Black
1	_____	_____	_____	White
2	_____	_____	_____	White
3	_____	_____	_____	White
4	_____	_____	_____	White
5	_____	_____	_____	White
Total	_____	_____	_____	White

*See Exercise 10 for an explanation of how to calculate percent deviation.

2. Selection for Size

Trial	No. Squares Selected		
	1″	½″	¼″
1	_____	_____	_____
2	_____	_____	_____
3	_____	_____	_____
4	_____	_____	_____
5	_____	_____	_____
6	_____	_____	_____
7	_____	_____	_____
8	_____	_____	_____
9	_____	_____	_____
10	_____	_____	_____
11	_____	_____	_____
Total	_____	_____	_____

Note: As with problem 1, percent deviation can be calculated for the above data.

Name _____ Class _____ Date _____

3. Selection for Color and Size

Trial	No. Squares Selected					
	1″ black	½″ black	¼″ black	1″ white	½″ white	¼″ white
1	_____	_____	_____	_____	_____	_____
2	_____	_____	_____	_____	_____	_____
3	_____	_____	_____	_____	_____	_____
4	_____	_____	_____	_____	_____	_____
5	_____	_____	_____	_____	_____	_____
6	_____	_____	_____	_____	_____	_____
7	_____	_____	_____	_____	_____	_____
8	_____	_____	_____	_____	_____	_____
9	_____	_____	_____	_____	_____	_____
10	_____	_____	_____	_____	_____	_____
11	_____	_____	_____	_____	_____	_____
Total	_____	_____	_____	_____	_____	_____

Note: As with problem 1, percent deviation can be calculated for the above data.

Exercise 14

Relative Fitness and Selection Coefficients

In the state of genetic equilibrium it is assumed that, among other things, all matings are equally fertile. In other words, the possessors of all genotypes contribute equally to the gene pool of the next generation. However, in most real situations the contribution of the various genotypes varies.

Natural selection refers to differences in fertility among the various genotypes. The term *fitness* is used to describe the contribution of each genotype to the next generation's gene pool. Thus, natural selection can be described by measuring the fitness of the different genotypes in the population.

The simplest situation is when selection is complete against a particular genotype. In this situation, possessors of the genotype in question produce no offspring because of their high mortality, infertility, etc., and are said to have a fitness of zero.

Example The fitness of the homozygous recessive genotype, *aa*, is 0 while the *relative fitness* of *AA* and *Aa*, whose phenotypes are indistinguishable, is set at 1. Relative fitness refers to the relationship among the fitness values of the genotypes, with the highest fitness usually arbitrarily set at 1.

In this example $[A] = p = 0.5$ and $[a] = q = 0.5$. Therefore, $[AA] = p^2 = 0.25$, $[Aa] = 2pq = 0.50$, and $[aa] = q^2 = 0.25$. Since the relative fitness of *aa* is 0, the effective breeding population is composed only of genotypes *AA* and *Aa*. In this breeding population

$$[AA] = \frac{p^2}{p^2 + 2pq} = \frac{0.25}{0.5 + 0.25} = 0.33$$

and

$$[Aa] = \frac{2pq}{p^2 + 2pq} = \frac{0.5}{0.5 + 0.25} = 0.67$$

We then can list all possible matings and determine the frequencies of offspring as follows:

Mating Type	Frequency	Frequency Offspring		
		AA	Aa	aa
AA × AA	$(0.33)^2 = 0.11$	0.11		
AA × Aa	$2(0.33)(0.67) = 0.44$	0.22	0.22	
Aa × Aa	$(0.67)^2 = 0.45$	0.11	0.22	0.11
		0.44	0.44	0.11*

*This line adds up to 0.99 instead of 1.00 because we have rounded off our answers.

Note that in this table the frequency of the genotype aa has dropped from 0.25 to 0.11. The frequency of Aa also has dropped, although the number of heterozygous individuals in the populaton is still high.

The strength of selective pressure is measured by the *selection coefficient(s)*. The relationship between relative fitness (RF) and the selection coefficient is given by the formula $RF = 1 - s$. RF values can be determined from fertility and mortality data. Here we are interested in the numbers of offspring actually produced by the possessors of differing genotypes. From the selection coefficient we can calculate changes in gene and genotypic frequencies over the generations.

When selection is complete against a dominant allele, the resulting frequencies are very different from those seen in the case of selection against a recessive. In such a situation the breeding population is composed entirely of aa individuals. Since aa individuals cannot produce AA or Aa offspring, the frequencies of these latter genotypes will drop to zero in a single generation. New cases of A will result from *mutation*. Thus, in any consideration of a real situation, the *mutation rate* must be considered, along with the selection coefficient.

The situation becomes more complex when the three genotypes have distinct phenotypic expressions associated with different selection coefficients. In the case of *balanced polymorphism*, the heterozygous genotype may have the highest relative fitness. However, it is not our purpose here to pursue these more complicated situations.

PROBLEMS
1. In the example used above, the frequency of *aa* dropped from 0.25 to 0.11 in a single generation. Taking the F_1* gene pool, and assuming no mutation, what will be the change in the frequency of *aa* in the next generation? Is the amount of change the same between the P and F_1 generations as it is between the F_1 and F_2 generations? If not, which difference is greatest? What differences are there in the proportion of *a* found in the homozygous and heterozygous genotypes in the first, second, and third generations?

2. Repeat the above calculations using a relative fitness of 0.5 for the *aa* genotype. How do these results compare with those of problem 1?

ANSWERS
1. The effective breeding population in the F_1 generation is composed of *AA* and *Aa* individuals. The relative proportions of these genotypes are

$$[AA] = \frac{0.44}{0.44 + 0.44} = 0.5 \quad \text{and} \quad [aa] = \frac{0.44}{0.44 + 0.44} = 0.5$$

We can then construct the following table:

		Frequency Offspring		
Mating Type	**Frequency**	**AA**	**Aa**	**aa**
AA × AA	$(0.5)^2 = 0.25$	0.25		
AA × Aa	$2(0.5)(0.5) = 0.5$	0.25	0.25	
Aa × Aa	$(0.5)^2 = 0.25$	0.06	0.13	0.06
		0.56	0.38	0.06

*The letter P refers to the parental generation, F_1 to the first descending (filial) generation, and F_2 to the second descending generation.

Relative Fitness and Selection Coefficients

The frequency of aa has dropped only 0.05 between generations F_1 and F_2, as compared to a drop of 0.14 between generations P and F_1. If further calculations are made, it will be seen that the change in frequency will become less and less. At the same time, the proportion of recessive alleles in the heterozygous condition will increase.

2. In this situation the breeding population is composed of AA, Aa, and one-half of the aa individuals (which is the same as saying all aa individuals produce one-half as many offspring). The effective breeding population can be calculated as follows:

$$[AA] = \frac{0.25}{0.25 + 0.5 + 0.125} = 0.29$$

$$[Aa] = \frac{0.5}{0.25 + 0.5 + 0.125} = 0.57$$

$$[aa] = \frac{0.125}{0.25 + 0.5 + 0.125} = 0.14$$

		Frequency Offspring		
Mating Types	Frequency	AA	Aa	aa
AA × AA	$(0.29)^2 = 0.08$	0.08		
AA × Aa	$2(0.29)(0.57) = 0.33$	0.17	0.17	
AA × aa	$2(0.29)(0.14) = 0.08$		0.08	
Aa × Aa	$(0.57)^2 = 0.32$	0.08	0.16	0.08
Aa × aa	$2(0.57)(0.14) = 0.16$		0.08	0.08
aa × aa	$(0.14)^2 = 0.02$			0.02
		0.33	0.49	0.18

In this case, the frequency of aa has dropped from 0.25 to 0.18. You might want to carry this on for an additional generation.

SUGGESTED READING

Cook, L. M. *Coefficients of Natural Selection*. London: Hutchinson University Library, 1971.

Exercise 15

Statistical Analysis of Phenotypic Variation

In attempting to understand the nature of human variation, physical anthropologists visit different human populations and collect phenotypic data which can then be compared. Some of the traits studied are determined primarily by simply genetic mechanisms. Some of these were discussed in Exercise 1. But the vast majority of human characteristics result from the interplay of genetic, environmental, and socio-cultural factors.

This and the next two exercises will study various kinds of variation. Exercise 16 will deal with *anthropometry*, the measurements of the human body, and Exercise 17 discusses *dermatoglyphics*, which includes the study of fingerprint patterns. This exercise will study several phenotypic variants and will present methods for their analysis.

PROBLEMS

1. The first step is the collection of phenotypic data. There are a great number of traits which can be studied. Select one trait from among the following: distance attained for standing or running broad jump, pulse rate, stature, or (if equipment is available) blood pressure, grip strength, or vital capacity.

After you have selected a trait for study, select a sample for study. This sample can be members of your class, a group of children, and so forth. Your sample should include at least ten individuals. Measure the trait in your sample and enter the values on the chart on page 109.

2. Statistics is a tool that allows us to deal precisely with information. The main function of statistics is to summarize data by means of various calculations. There are a great number of ways to deal with data, and this exercise will discuss only a few.

One of the most basic methods of summarizing data is to calculate an average or *mean*. The mean provides a single value which is used to represent the entire distribution of a specific set of figures. It is defined as the sum of the individual values divided by the number of values. The formula is written

$$\overline{X} = \frac{\Sigma X}{N}$$

where $\overline{X}$ = mean
  Σ = sum
  X = value of case
  N = number of cases

Calculate the mean for your data. Enter the mean on the chart.

3. The *standard deviation* is a measure of variation. It tells us the degree to which the values in a set of values vary from the mean. Standard deviation is calculated from the formula

$$s = \sqrt{\frac{\Sigma x^2}{N - 1}}$$

where s = standard deviation
  Σx^2 = sum of the squares of the deviation of each value from the mean

Study the following example and then calculate the standard deviations for your sample.

Example

X	$\overline{X}$	x	x²
35	32	3	9
28	32	4	16
37	32	5	25
29	32	3	9
32	32	0	0
37	32	5	25
34	32	2	4
28	32	4	16
29	32	3	9
31	32	1	1
$\Sigma X = 320$			$\Sigma x^2 = 114$

$$\overline{X} = \frac{\Sigma X}{N} = \frac{320}{10} = 32$$

$$s = \sqrt{\frac{\Sigma x^2}{N - 1}} = \sqrt{\frac{114}{9}} = \sqrt{12.7} = 3.6$$

$$\overline{X} \pm 1s = 32 \pm 3.6 = 35.6 \text{ to } 28.4$$

Exercise 15

What does the value of s mean? In the most general terms, the greater the size of the standard deviation, the greater the variation within the data. So, for example, a value of s of 5.6 for a specific set of data would mean that there was greater variation within those data than within a set of data with an s of 3.8. The value of s is called *one standard deviation*. So, if s is calculated to be 2.6, this would represent one standard deviation, 5.2 would be two standard deviations, 7.8 three standard deviations, and so on. For most biological data the mean ($\overline{X}$) plus or minus ($\pm$) one standard deviation will include 68.26 percent of the data, $X \pm 2s$ will include 95.54 percent, and $\overline{X} \pm 3s$ will include 99.73 percent.

4. In Exercise 10 we studied the problem of sampling error. In the present study we also must be concerned with sampling error. If our sample is small, our mean may differ significantly from the mean of a larger population simply because, by chance, our small sample included individuals who differed greatly from the mean of the larger population. To estimate how reliable our sample is, we can use the *standard error of the mean,* which is calculated from the following formula:

$$s_{\overline{x}} = \frac{s}{\sqrt{N}}$$

where $s_{\overline{x}}$ = standard error of the mean
$\quad s$ = standard deviation
$\quad N$ = size of our sample

As an example we can calculate the standard error of the mean using the example from problem 3.

$$s_{\overline{x}} = \frac{s}{\sqrt{N}} = \frac{3.6}{\sqrt{10}} = 1.1$$

What does this value mean? It is interpreted in much the same way as the standard deviation. In our example the mean plus and minus one standard error of the mean defines a range of values from 2.5 to 4.7. This can be interpreted as meaning that the probability is 68 out of 100 that the mean of the population from which our sample was drawn falls between 2.5 and 4.7. Looking at the formula, we can see that the larger the sample size, the smaller will be the standard error of the mean, that is to say, the more reliable is our sample.

Calculate the standard error of the mean for your sample.

5. An interesting exercise would be to divide your sample into two smaller ones, one male and one female, and to see if there is a significant difference between females and males in their heart rates, blood pressures, and so forth. Calculate the mean and standard deviation for each group. Then compare the means. There is a major problem in interpretation when the means are compared. The differences in means can be due to sample error, or they can be due to a real difference existing between the two groups. There are several methods of handling significance statistically, but these methods go beyond the scope of this workbook.

SUGGESTED READINGS

Kennedy, K. A. R. *Human Variation in Space and Time.* Dubuque, Iowa: Wm. C. Brown, 1976.

Stini, W. A. *Ecology and Human Adaptations.* Dubuque, Iowa: Wm. C. Brown, 1975.

Underwood, J. H. *Biocultural Interactions and Human Variation.* Dubuque, Iowa: Wm. C. Brown, 1975.

Name _____ Class _____ Date _____

_____

Trait _____ $N =$ _____

Values:

_____ _____ _____ _____

_____ _____ _____ _____

_____ _____ _____ _____

_____ _____ _____ _____

_____ _____ _____ _____

Mean = _____

Standard deviation = _____

Standard error of the mean = _____

_____

Exercise 16

Anthropometry

Anthropometry involves the measurement of the human body. It provides us, first, with data concerning the variability of the human species and, second, with data which can be put to practical use in such areas as developing size categories in clothing, designing cockpits and consoles in airplanes or seating in automobiles, and other fields in which precise body measurements are needed.

This exercise deals with only a few of the possible measurements that can be taken. Anthropometric equipment is specialized and expensive. Here, inexpensive and easily obtainable instruments, such as metric tape measures (one calibrated in inches can do) and sliding calipers, will be used. Measurements should be taken in millimeters or inches.

The following measurements are to be taken with the metric tape:

1. Head circumference   The tape should pass above the brow ridge but should not include it.

Figure 16-1 Head circumference.

2. Sagittal arc The tape is placed in the midsagittal plane, that is, on a line from the nose, between the eyes, to the middle of the back of the head, which bisects the head into two equal parts. Measure from the landmark known as the *glabella* on the forehead (it is located between the brow ridges above the eyes) to the *nuchale landmark* at the base of the *occiput.* (The occiput is the lower back of the skull. At the base of the occiput you should be able to feel the nuchale landmark, a small ridge.)

3. Bitragion-coronal arc Pass the tape over the top of the head from the right tragion to the left tragion. The *tragion* is the cartilaginous notch just in front of the upper edge of the ear hole.

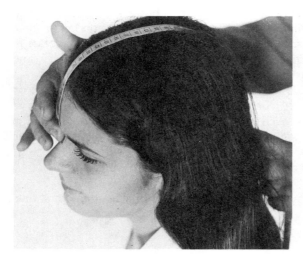

Figure 16-2 Sagittal arc.

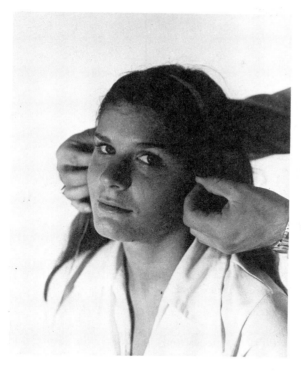

Figure 16-3 Bitragion-coronal arc.

The following measurements are to be made with the sliding caliper:

4. Nasal breadth Measure the maximum distance between the wings of the nostrils.

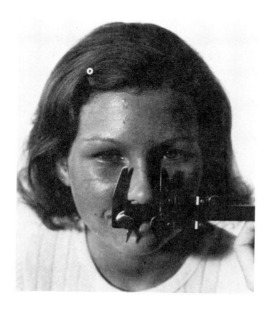

Figure 16-4 Nasal breadth.

Anthropometry

Figure 16-5 Nasal height.

5. Nasal height Measure the length of the nose from the *nasion,* the depression at the top of the nose, to the *subnasale,* the lowest point of the nose between the two nostrils.

From these last two measurements, 4 and 5, we can calculate the *nasal index.* The formula for the nasal index is

$$\frac{\text{Nasal breadth}}{\text{Nasal height}} \times 100$$

Take the series of five measurements on at least twelve people. Record the data on the following chart, including the nasal index, which you can calculate from your data.

Name _____ Class _____ Date _____

Anthropometric Data

Sex	Age	1	2	3	4	5	Nasal Index
___	___	___	___	___	___	___	___
___	___	___	___	___	___	___	___
___	___	___	___	___	___	___	___
___	___	___	___	___	___	___	___
___	___	___	___	___	___	___	___
___	___	___	___	___	___	___	___
___	___	___	___	___	___	___	___
___	___	___	___	___	___	___	___
___	___	___	___	___	___	___	___
___	___	___	___	___	___	___	___
___	___	___	___	___	___	___	___
___	___	___	___	___	___	___	___
___	___	___	___	___	___	___	___
___	___	___	___	___	___	___	___
___	___	___	___	___	___	___	___
___	___	___	___	___	___	___	___
___	___	___	___	___	___	___	___

PROBLEMS

1. Divide your sample by sex and for each sex work out the *mean* and *standard deviation* for the measurements taken. (See Exercise 15 for discussion of the mean and the standard deviation.) What differences do you note?

2. Divide your sample in other ways. For example, you might want to compare athletes to nonathletes. In these cases, are there differences in the mean and the standard deviation?

SUGGESTED READINGS

Montagu, M. F. A. *A Handbook of Anthropometry.* Springfield, Ill.: Charles C Thomas, 1960.

Olivier, G. *Practical Anthropology.* Springfield, Ill.: Charles C Thomas, 1969.

Exercise 17

Dermatoglyphics

One way in which individuals as well as populations differ from each other is in the pattern of *epidermal ridges* on the fingers, palms, toes, and soles of the feet. The study of these patterns is called *dermatoglyphics*. Here we will focus on the most commonly studied area of epidermal ridges, the fingertips.

Fingerprint patterns develop in the eighteenth week of fetal life and do not change thereafter. The pattern is almost the same in identical twins, but the fact that it does vary somewhat indicates that early environmental influences also are involved. The exact mode of inheritance is not known at this time. However, similarities in certain aspects of the patterns reflect closeness of genetic relationship.

There are two commonly used ways of describing fingerprints. The first is by the overall pattern (see Figure 17-1). The simplest pattern is the *arch*, composed of lines curving upward. A *loop* is U-shaped, with the open end of the U directed toward one side of the finger and the base of the U intersected by a line that creates a triangular intersection known as a *triradius*. A *whorl* is an enclosed circle with two triradii at its base. Note in the figure the basic variants of the arch, loop and whorl, and the triradii.

The second way of describing fingerprints is by counting ridges between a triradius and the center of a loop or whorl. Since a simple arch has no triradii, it will have a *ridge count* of zero. Tented arches also have ridge counts of zero. With a whorl, where there are two triradii, the count that produces the highest number of ridges is most often used. See Figure 17-1 for examples. A count is made on each of the ten fingers. The separate counts are then added together to give the *total ridge count*.

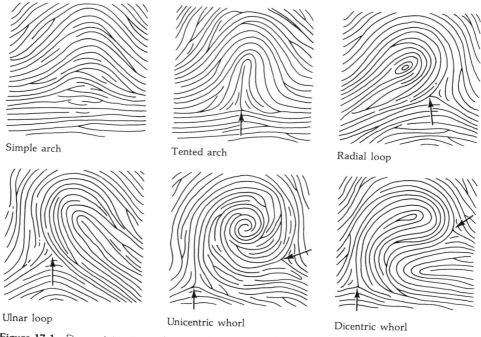

Simple arch   Tented arch   Radial loop

Ulnar loop   Unicentric whorl   Dicentric whorl

Figure 17-1   Fingerprint patterns. Arrows point to the triradii.

The total ridge count can vary greatly. A range of from 0 to 285 was found in one English sample.[1] The percentages of arches, loops, and whorls also differ greatly among populations. For example, Europeans average between 63 and 73 percent loops, whereas the Australian aborigines average between 28 and 46 percent.[2]

In the following exercise you will need a black ink pad and a low-power magnifying glass. The fingerprint should be made directly on the recording form. To take your fingerprint, place each finger, one at a time, lightly on the ink pad and roll the finger from one side to the other on the paper in the appropriate space. After the fingerprints have been made, classify each print as to overall pattern. If actual fingerprinting equipment is available, the prints will be clear enough to obtain ridge counts.

[1]C. S. Coon, *The Living Races of Man* (New York: Knopf, 1965), p. 258.

[2]Ibid., p. 261.

Dermatoglyphics

Name _____ Class _____ Date _____

Individual Fingerprint Analysis

Sex _____

Record your fingerprints below:

Right thumb   *1st finger*   *2d finger*   *3d finger*   *4th finger*

Left thumb   *1st finger*   *2d finger*   *3d finger*   *4th finger*

Right Hand			Left Hand		
Digit	Type	Ridge Count	Digit	Type	Ridge Count
Thumb	_____	_____	Thumb	_____	_____
1st finger	_____	_____	1st finger	_____	_____
2d finger	_____	_____	2d finger	_____	_____
3d finger	_____	_____	3d finger	_____	_____
4th finger	_____	_____	4th finger	_____	_____

Total number of simple arches _____

Total number of tented arches _____

Total number of radial loops _____

Total number of ulnar loops _____

Total number of unicentric whorls _____

Total number of dicentric whorls _____

Total number of arches _____, loops _____, whorls _____

Total ridge count _____

PROBLEMS

Collect data from the class and answer the following questions.

1. What is the range of variation in the class in the number of arches, loops, and whorls? Compare the average number and the range of arches, loops, and whorls for males and females. Do you see any differences?

2. If ridge counts were obtained, what is the range of variation in the class in the total ridge count? Compare the average number and range in total ridge count for males and females. Do you see any differences?

If possible, analyze the fingerprints of several members of your family. Then answer the following questions.

3. Determine the range of variation in the number of arches, loops, and whorls and the total ridge count among members of your immediate family, as well as the range of variation and the average number for your more distant relatives. In general, do the data from your relatives conform more closely to your own fingerprints than to the data from the class as a whole?

Dermatoglyphics

4. Do the members of your immediate family show a ridge count closer to yours than more distant relatives (uncles, aunts, cousins)?

5. What generalizations can you make?

SUGGESTED READINGS

American Journal of Physical Anthropology, 42 (March 1975). The entire issue is devoted to articles on dermatoglyphics.

Cummins, H., and C. Midlo. *Fingerprints, Palms and Soles.* New York: Dover, 1961.

Penrose, L. S. "Dermatoglyphics," *Scientific American,* 221 (December 1969), 72–84.

Exercise 18

Growth and Development

Ontogeny is the study of growth and development. Differences in ontogeny exist among different populations. While it is not practical in this workbook to compare ontogenetic factors in differing populations, this exercise is given as an introduction to some of the general concepts in the field.

This exercise deals with the growth of the body. It has often been noted that different parts of the body develop at differing rates. Here you will have the opportunity to document some of these differences.

PROBLEM

Take a series of four measurements on individuals of differing ages. Ideally, several infants and children of varying ages, some teen-agers, adults, and at least one older person should be included in the sample. Of course, you may be limited in the type of sample which you can obtain, but try to get as large a sample as you can.

Have the subject stand upright against a wall or door and, using a tape measure or yardstick, take the following measurements. Use the metric system if possible. A baby will have to be measured in a prone position. The four measurements are:

1. Distance from top of head to top of shoulder
2. Distance from top of shoulder to hip (use the bony projection of the hip bone as the point of measurement)
3. Distance from hip to floor (bottom of feet)
4. Distance from the shoulder to tip of index finger

Also, measure the total height, which will be the sum of measurements 1, 2, and 3. Record these figures in the proper column on the accompanying chart, along with the subject's sex and age.

Using the data you have collected, calculate the percentage of the total height for each of the three measures 1 to 3. For example, if the subject is 68 inches tall with a head height (1) of 11 inches, the head height makes up 16.2 percent of the total stature. Do the same for measurements 2 and 3.

In addition, calculate the relative length of the arms and legs by using the following formula:

$$\frac{\text{Length of arm (4)}}{\text{Length of leg (3)}} \times 100$$

An index of 100 means that the arms and legs are of equal length, while an index of 50 indicates that the legs are twice as long as the arms.

After all the calculations have been made, compare each type of calculation with differences in age. What conclusions can you draw about changes in proportion with increasing age? You might want to show the changes in relative proportion on a graph.

SUGGESTED READINGS

Cammon, R. W. *Human Growth and Development.* Springfield, Ill.: Charles C Thomas, 1970.

Malina, R. M. *Growth and Development: The First Twenty Years in Man.* Minneapolis: Burgess, 1975.

Ontogenetic Data

Age	Sex	Total Height	1	2	3	4	%1	%2	%3	Arm/Leg Index

Exercise 19

The Postcranial Skeleton

Before beginning a comparative study of various primate skeletons, you must become familiar with the different bones which make up the skeleton. This exercise deals with the *postcranial* skeleton. (The skull will be studied in detail in Exercise 20.)

On the following pages you will find drawings of the monkey skeleton and the human skeleton, which will be used in this exercise. Note that each bone is numbered and identified in the key. Attempt to locate these bones on an actual skeleton.

AXIAL SKELETON

Skull The skull consists of twenty-two separate bones which we will discuss in Exercise 20.

Vertebral column The vertebral column, or *spine,* is composed of several elements, or *vertebrae.* The number of vertebrae differs among the different primates, with thirty-three in humans. The vertebral column can be divided into various regions: *cervical, thoracic, lumbar, sacrum,* and *caudal* (*coccyx* in humans).

Ribs and sternum The rib cage is composed of the *ribs,* which are attached posteriorly to the *thoracic vertebrae* and anteriorly to the *sternum.*

APPENDICULAR SKELETON

Shoulder girdle The upper limbs attach to the trunk by means of the shoulder girdle. The *clavicle* articulates with the sternum and the *scapula.*

Arm The upper arm consists of the *humerus.* The lower arm consists of two bones, the larger *ulna* and the smaller *radius.*

Wrist   The wrist is made up of the eight *carpal bones.*

Hand   The hand is composed of five *metacarpal bones* and fourteen *phalanges,* two in the thumb and three in each of the other fingers.

Pelvic girdle   The pelvic girdle is composed of two elements, the sacrum and the two *innominate bones.* At birth, each innominate bone is made up of three separate bones which later fuse. But the names of these three bones are used to designate the three areas of the adult pelvis: the *ilium, ischium,* and *pubis.*

Leg   The upper leg consists of the *femur,* the longest bone in the body. The lower leg consists of the larger *tibia* and the smaller *fibula.* The bone in the knee is the *patella.*

Ankle   The ankle is composed of the seven *tarsal bones.*

Foot   The foot is composed of five *metatarsal bones* and fourteen phalanges.

Key for Figures 19-1 and 19-2

1. Skull	14. Carpals
2. Cervical vertebrae	15. Metacarpals
3. Thoracic vertebrae	16. Phalanges
4. Lumbar vertebrae	17. Ilium
5. Sacrum	18. Ischium
6. Caudal vertebrae	19. Pubis
(coccyx in humans)	20. Femur
7. Ribs	21. Patella
8. Sternum	22. Tibia
9. Clavicle	23. Fibula
10. Scapula	24. Tarsals
11. Humerus	25. Metatarsals
12. Ulna	26. Phalanges
13. Radius	

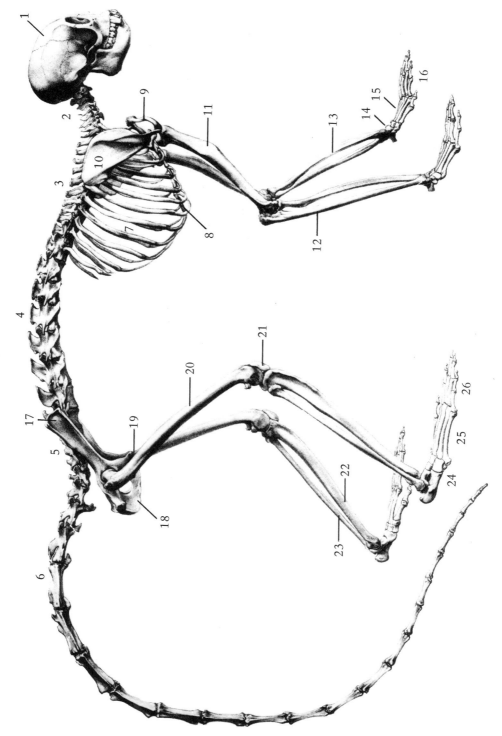

Figure 19-1 Skeleton of an Old World monkey, *Miopithecus talapoin*.

131

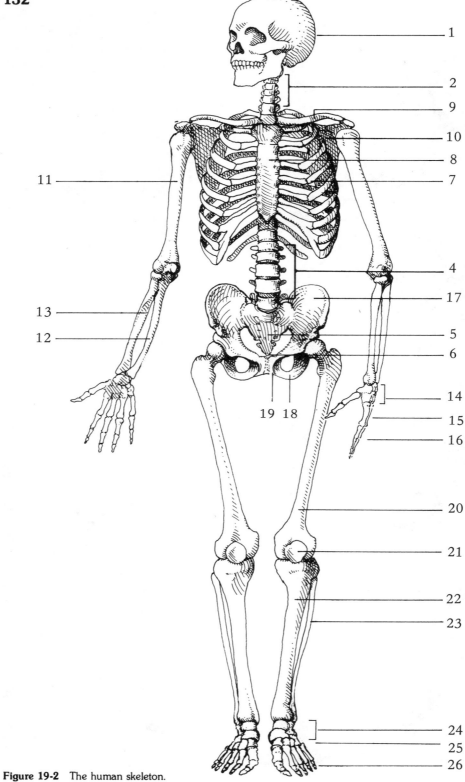

Figure 19-2 The human skeleton.

In discussing anatomy, several terms are used to describe the location of anatomical features. In the diagram of the quadrupedal vertebrate (Figure 19-3) the four basic positions are defined. They are:

Anterior Toward the front of the body

Posterior Toward the back of the body

Dorsal Toward the top of the body

Ventral Toward the bottom of the body

However, in anatomical descriptions the human body is positioned in an upright posture. Thus, the anatomical references for a human body differ from those for a quadrupedal body. The most important anatomical reference terms are defined below and are located on the diagrams in Figure 19-4.

Anterior Toward the front of the body

Posterior Toward the rear of the body

Midsagittal plane The plane which divides the body longitudinally and passes through the center of the body

Medial Toward the midsagittal plane

Lateral Away from the midsagittal plane

Proximal Near the point of central attachment

Distal Far from the point of central attachment

Superior Lying above another point

Inferior Lying below another point

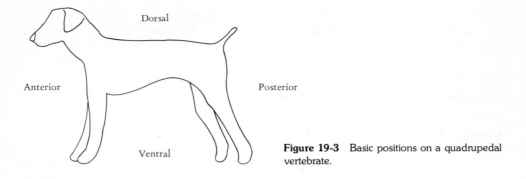

Figure 19-3 Basic positions on a quadrupedal vertebrate.

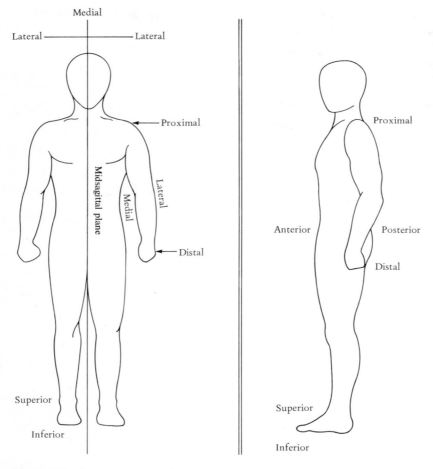

Figure 19-4 Basic positions in a human.

Exercise 19

Exercise 20

The Skull

The normal human adult skull is composed of twenty-two distinct bones. Learning the names and features of all of these is not necessary for our purposes. In this exercise you will learn some of the basic information about the skull, which will aid in discussions of comparative anatomy of the skull and in the analysis of fossil finds.

The skull consists of the *cranium* and the *mandible.* The mandible is the lower jaw, which articulates with the rest of the skull, or cranium. The cranium can be divided into the *face* and *calvaria,* which contains the brain.

The following is a list of the major bones of the skull, which should be located on the drawing of the human skull. After this list is a list of major features (page 138), which should also be located. Note that each bone and feature is numbered and identified in the key.

The major bones of the skull are:

Frontal   A bone forming the forehead, roof of the orbits, and the front portion of the skull vault

Parietal   A pair of bones lying behind the frontal and forming a major part of the skull walls

Occipital   A bone lying behind the parietals and forming the back and basal portion of the skull.

Temporal   A pair of bones lying beneath the parietals, above and in front of the occipital, forming the major part of the skull walls

Maxillary   A pair of bones forming the upper jaw, containing the teeth, enclosing the nasal cavity, forming part of the floor of the orbits and the anterior portion of the roof of the mouth

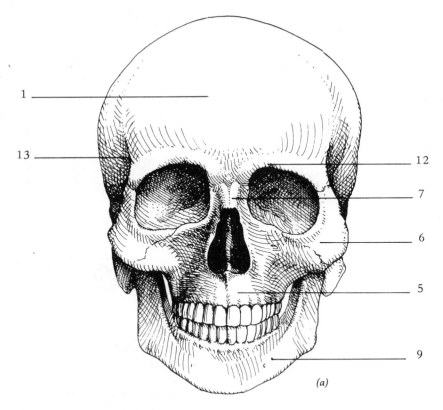

Figure 20-1 The human skull: (a) front, (b) side, (c) bottom.

Key

1. Frontal
2. Parietal
3. Occipital
4. Temporal
5. Maxillary
6. Zygomatic
7. Nasal
8. Palatine
9. Mandible
10. Foramen magnum
11. Occipital condyles
12. Supraorbital torus
13. Postorbital constriction
14. Mastoid process
15. Zygomatic arch

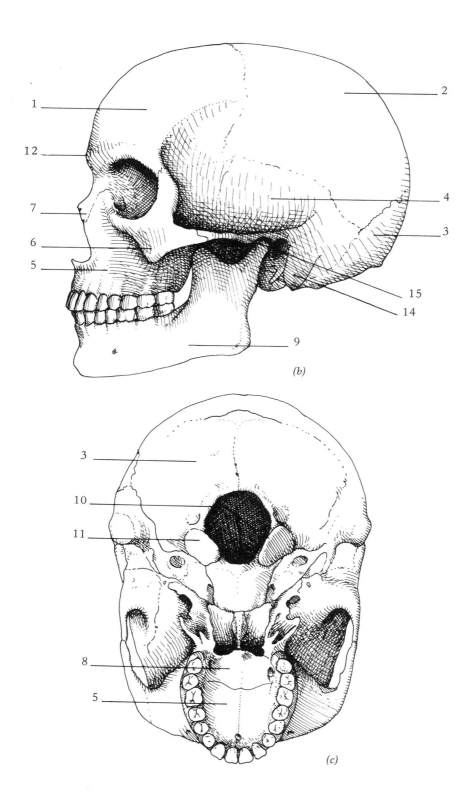

(b)

(c)

Zygomatic   A pair of bones lying in the lateral portion of the face, forming a part of the lateral walls of the orbits and extending partway back to form part of the zygomatic arch

Nasal   A pair of bones forming the bridge of the nose above the nasal cavity

Palatine   A pair of bones forming the posterior portion of the roof of the mouth

Mandible   the lower jaw

Some of the major *features* of the human skull are:

Foramen magnum   The large opening in the base of the occipital

Occipital condyles   Two ovoid processes on each side of the foramen magnum which articulate with the top of the spine

Supraorbital torus   A shelflike projection of bone above the orbits called the *brow ridge*

Postorbital constriction   Constriction of the brain case immediately behind the orbits

Mastoid process   Large, downward-projecting processes behind and below the ear opening

Zygomatic arch   Two slender bridges of bone composed of the backward projection of the zygomatic bone and the forward projection of the temporal bone

Exercise 21

Osteometry

Osteometry is the study of measurements of skeletal materials. In this exercise we shall restrict the discussion to measurements of the human skull. Some of the methods used for sexing and aging skeletal materials employ osteometric methods (see Exercises 22 and 23). Osteometric measurements and the indices which can be calculated from them can be important in archaeological, paleoanthropological (see Exercise 37), *forensic,* human variation, and genetic studies.

PROBLEMS

1. Figure 21-1 shows the outline of a skull from the front and side with certain landmarks named and shown. Using these landmarks, draw the following lines directly on the drawings:
   a. *Bizygomatic width:* Draw the line from the right to the left *zygion.*
   b. *Total facial height:* Draw the line from the *nasion* to the *gnathion.*
   c. *Upper facial height:* Draw the line from the *nasion* to the *prosthion* (superior alveolar point).
   d. *Cranial breadth:* Draw the line from right to left *euryon.*
   e. *Cranial length:* Draw the line from the *glabella* to the *opisthocranion.*
   f. *Cranial height:* Draw the line from the *porion* to the *bregma.* (Cranial height is more commonly based on the distance from the *basion* to the bregma. The basion, which is the most forward point on the rim of the foramen magnum, is not visible in the drawings.)

2. There are many indices that anthropologists use in doing comparative osteometric studies. We shall look at four of these.
   a. Using a ruler, measure the six lines which were drawn in problem 1. Enter these measurements (in millimeters) on the chart on page 141.

b. Calculate the following indices and record them on the chart:

$$\text{Total facial index} = \frac{\text{total facial height}}{\text{bizygomatic width}} \times 100$$

$$\text{Upper facial index} = \frac{\text{upper facial height}}{\text{bizygomatic width}} \times 100$$

$$\text{Cranial index} = \frac{\text{cranial breadth}}{\text{cranial length}} \times 100$$

$$\text{Height-length index} = \frac{\text{cranial height}}{\text{cranial length}} \times 100$$

3. What exactly do these indices tell us? For each index you calculate, what would be the result of an increase or reduction of 10?

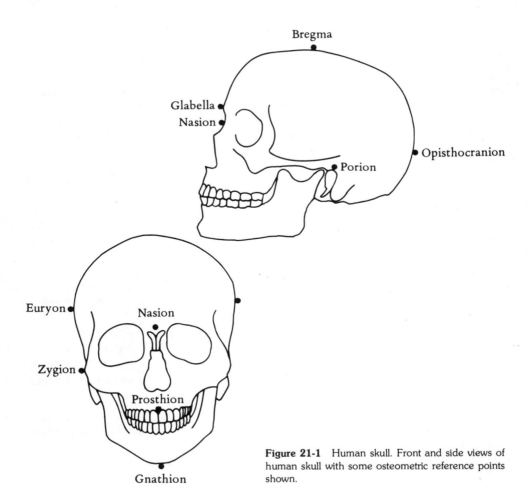

Figure 21-1 Human skull. Front and side views of human skull with some osteometric reference points shown.

Name _____ Class _____ Date _____

Measurements (mm)
  Bizygomatic width   _____

  Total facial height   _____

  Upper facial height   _____

  Cranial breadth   _____

  Cranial length   _____

  Cranial height   _____

Indices
  Total facial index   _____

  Upper facial index   _____

  Cranial index   _____

  Height-length index   _____

Note If the measurements mentioned in this exercise are to be taken on real skulls, the proper equipment must be used. For some of the measurements the skulls must be placed in specific configurations in order to get accurate measurements. See the books mentioned in the Suggested Readings for details on how to take measurements on actual skeletal material and also for a more comprehensive list of measurements and indices.

ANSWERS

2. Total facial index   = 97
Upper facial index   = 58
Cranial index   = 83
Height-length index = 63

3. The indices tell us the relationship between two measurements. For example, the cranial index tells us the relationship between the breadth and length of the skull. Since these indices are all under 100, human skulls are longer than wide. But the lower the number, the greater is the length of the skull relative to its width. The cranial index is used to classify skulls into three categories: *dolichocranic* (below 74.9), *mesocranic* (75 to 79.9), and *brachycranic* (80.0 and above). For all indices, as the number decreases, the relative measure of the denominator increases with respect to the measure of the numerator. The reverse is true as the number increases.

SUGGESTED READINGS

Kelso, J., and G. Ewing. *Introduction to Physical Anthropology Laboratory Manual.* Boulder, Colo.: Pruett Press, 1962. See laboratory units 2 and 3.

Oliver, G. *Practical Anthropology.* Springfield, Ill.: Charles C Thomas, 1969. See chaps. 8, 9, and 17.

Wetherington, R. K. *Laboratory Exercises in Physical Anthropology.* Springfield, Ill.: Charles C Thomas, 1970. See exercise 8.

Exercise 22

Sexing Skeletal Material

Many anthropologists are directly or indirectly concerned with *osteological* remains. The analysis of skeletal materials is important in archaeological research, paleoanthropological studies, *forensic* investigations, and various genetic studies such as those on the degree and impact of gene flow between groups.

Different animal species display varying degrees of *sexual dimorphism,* which is the sum of the average differences between males and females of the same species. The sexual differences in the human skeleton are not absolute. There is no one characteristic that will definitely indicate whether a particular specimen is male or female. Even using a series of characteristics on complete skeletons, sexual determinations can never be considered 100 percent accurate. Some experienced investigators have tested their skills in determining sex on samples for which the sex of each individual was known but not disclosed to the researchers being "tested." Accuracies as high as 95 percent were reached by some when the total skeleton, adult pelvis alone, or one adult innominate alone was used. An 80 percent accuracy was the highest scored when the skull without mandible was used.[1]

The accuracy of any determination depends upon the following factors:

[1]W. M. Krogman, *The Human Skeleton in Forensic Medicine* (Springfield, Ill.: Charles C Thomas, 1962), pp. 112–113.

1. The completeness of the remains
2. If incomplete, which parts are available for study
3. The age at death (adult material is easier to sex than immature)
4. The presence or absence of bone pathologies
5. The presence or absence of cultural practices, such as head flattening by use of cradle boards, which alters the skeleton, and the recognition of such factors
6. The recognition of local adaptive variations in different populations
7. The experience of the investigator

In light of the above, you should realize that this exercise is simply meant to familiarize you with some of the more obvious distinctions in specimens which are "stereotypically" male and female in their characteristics. Also, we are only exploring the *inspection method* of sex determination, that is, determinations made on some-what subjective visual observations. Mathematical methods also exist which make use of precise measurements (see Suggested Readings).

The study of the vertebral column and appendages can give clues as to sexual identity. However, the most accurate determinations are based upon the skull and pelvis. This exercise will deal only with these parts of the skeleton. See Exercises 19 and 20 for the names of locations of bones and features of the skeleton.

Except for teeth, the skull and skull fragments are the most frequent parts of the skeleton uncovered in archaeology and human paleontology. Figure 22-1 shows many of the characteristics which can be used to distinguish the male from the female on the basis of the skull.

Of all skeletal parts, the pelvis shows the greatest degree of sexual dimorphism in humans. In large part, this is related to the adaptation of the female pelvis for childbirth.

Figure 22-2 shows a male and female pelvis from the front. The *ilia* in the female pelvis tends to flare out more and the *pelvic outlet* is usually broader than in the male. The *subpubic angle* in the male tends to be acute (V-shaped) when compared with that of the female, which is more U-shaped. In addition, the *pelvic cavity* is usually deeper in the male pelvis than in the female.

When viewed from the side, the *sciatic notch* tends to be wider in the female pelvis than in the male pelvis. Also, the inner surface of the *sacrum* is usually more vertical in the male pelvis. These features can be seen in Figure 22-3.

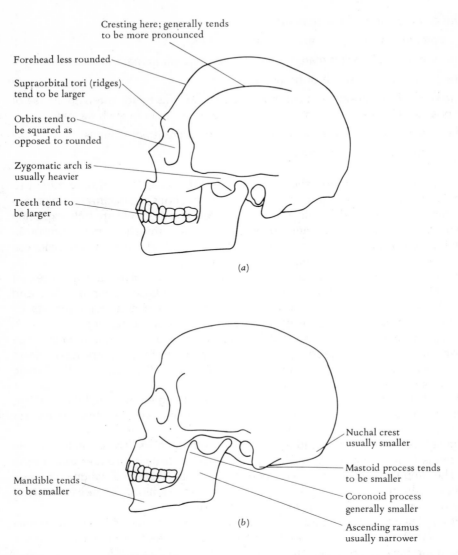

Cresting here; generally tends
to be more pronounced

Forehead less rounded

Supraorbital tori (ridges)
tend to be larger

Orbits tend to
be squared as
opposed to rounded

Zygomatic arch is
usually heavier

Teeth tend to
be larger

(a)

Nuchal crest
usually smaller

Mastoid process tends
to be smaller

Mandible tends
to be smaller

Coronoid process
generally smaller

Ascending ramus
usually narrower

(b)

Figure 22-1 Stereotypic (a) male skull and (b) female skull. Labels refer to comparisons between male and female skulls.

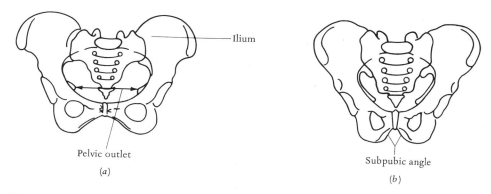

Figure 22-2 Front view of pelvis. (a) Stereotypic female pelvis. (b) Stereotypic male pelvis.

Figure 22-3 also shows differences in the details of the *pubis* and *ischium*. In the male pelvis the pubis is usually considerably shorter than the ischium, whereas in the female pelvis these areas are generally about the same length.

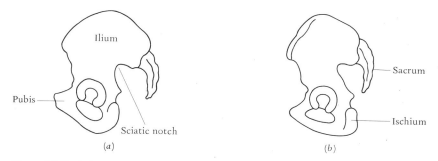

Figure 22-3 Side view of pelvis. (a) Stereotypic female pelvis. (b) Stereotypic male pelvis.

PROBLEM

Archaeologists and paleoanthropologists sometimes uncover burials which include the remains of more than one individual. Often various bones of these individuals have become mixed and have to be sorted out. In Figure 22-4 are several skulls and pelvises as well as parts of these two areas of the skeleton. They are all drawn so as to be stereotypically either male or female. Sort them out on the basis of sex and fill in the chart on page 149.

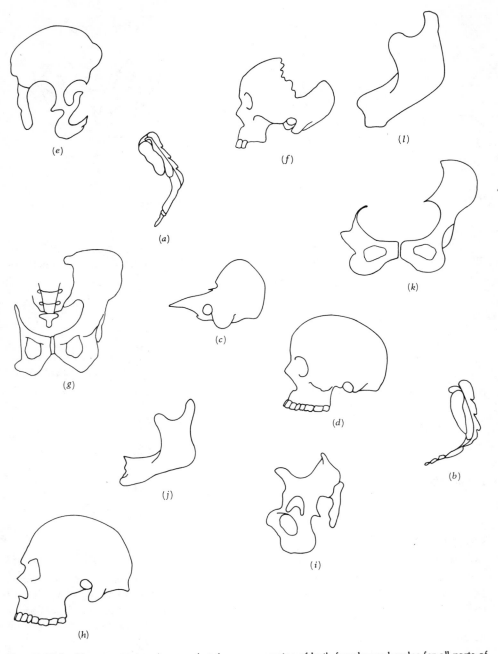

Figure 22-4 Human remains. Assume that there are remains of both females and males for all parts of the skeleton shown, so that your determinations will be based on comparison and analysis of relative differences.

Name _____ Class _____ Date _____

Specimen	Probable Sex	Reasons for Determination
a		
b		
c		
d		
e		
f		
g		
h		
i		
j		
k		
l		

ANSWERS

Males
	Reasons
b	Inner surface of sacrum more vertical than in *a*
c	Larger mastoid process and nuchal crest than in *d* or *f*
g	Subpubic angle V-shaped; pelvic inlet more constricted than in *k*
h	Larger mastoid process, nuchal crest, and supraorbital tori than in *d* or *f*; orbits squarer than *d* or *f*; forehead less rounded than *d* or *f*
i	Greater sciatic notch narrower than in *e*
l	Coronoid process larger and ascending ramus broader than in *j*

Females
	Reasons
a	Inner surface of sacrum is more angular than in *b*
d and *f*	Smaller mastoid process and nuchal crest than in *c*; smaller supraorbital tori, rounder orbits and more rounded forehead than in *h*
e	Greater sciatic notch wider than in *i*
j	Coronoid process smaller and ascending ramus narrower than in *l*
k	Subpubic angle U-shaped; pelvic inlet more rounded than in *g*

SUGGESTED READINGS

Kelso, J., and G. Ewing. *Introduction to Physical Anthropology Laboratory Manual.* Boulder, Colo.: Pruett Press, 1962. See laboratory unit 13.

Krogman, W. M. *The Human Skeleton in Forensic Medicine.* Springfield, Ill.: Charles C Thomas, 1962.

Exercise 23

Aging Skeletal Material

How many bones make up the human skeleton? The answer to this question depends on what stage of development the individual reaches before death. There are 806 bones in the eleven-week-old fetus, 450 bones at birth, and 206 bones in an adult.[1] Actually, these first two numbers more accurately represent centers of growth. That is, as the individual develops, various centers of bone growth meet and fuse, ultimately giving rise to a total of 206 bones. The sequence of bone fusions and of tooth eruptions can be used to estimate the age of an individual at death. It is generally more difficult to age a skeleton than to sex it. Also, the older the individual, the more difficult it is to make an accurate age determination.

Most bones begin as *cartilage*. The cartilage develops into bone through a complex process called *ossification*. Most adult long bones, such as the femur and humerus, have two or more centers of growth. The growth center of the shaft of a long bone is called the *diaphysis*. The growth centers at either end are called the *epiphyses* (Figure 23-1). As ossification continues, bone replaces more and more of the cartilage until the epiphyses and diaphysis merge and unite to form a single bone. Since *epiphyseal union,* as the above process is termed, occurs at different times in different bones, it can be used as one means of aging the skeleton up to the time when all unions have taken place, at about thirty years of age. The mean ages of epiphyseal union for several bones are given in Figure 23-2. However, it must be emphasized that there is a great deal of nonpathological variation in the age of epiphyseal union. One study shows, for example, the following range for the union of the proximal radial epiphysis: females 13 years to 19 years 10 months; males 14 years to 20 years 5 months.[2]

---

[1] W. M. Krogman, *The Human Skeleton in Forensic Medicine* (Springfield, Ill.: Charles C Thomas, 1962).

[2] Ibid., p. 35.

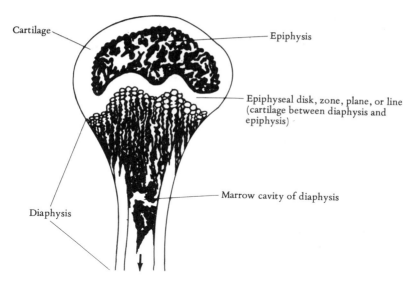

Figure 23-1 Growth of long bones. Schematic diagram of a longitudinal section through the upper end of a growing long bone.

The sequential eruption of the milk and permanent teeth is perhaps the best method of aging a skull of an individual under twenty years of age. The mean ages of tooth eruption of deciduous and permanent teeth are given in Figure 23-3.

PROBLEMS

1. Using the information in Figure 23-2 and the data provided in the following table, estimate the age range of individuals A, B, and C.

Individual (Average "White" Male)	Some Epiphyseal Unions That Have Occurred	Some Epiphyseal Unions That Have Not Occurred	Estimated Age Range
A	Distal humerus Distal radius Distal ulna	Proximal humerus Lateral clavicle	
B	Third phalanges of foot Metatarsals	Lesser trochanter (femur)	
C	Distal fibula Calcaneus	Distal femur	

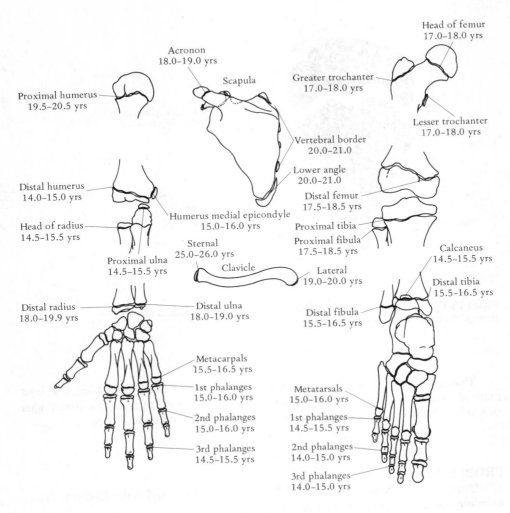

Figure 23-2 Age of epiphyseal union. The ages given are averages for "white" males.

2. Using the diagram of tooth eruption (Figure 23-3), write out the order of eruption of the deciduous dentition. Lowercase letters are used to refer to specific types of teeth, i for incisor, c for canine, and m for molar. The subscript indicates the exact tooth in the lower jaw, while the superscript is used for the upper jaw. Thus i_1 is the first lower deciduous incisor while m^2 is the second upper deciduous molar. (Since the chart shows only certain ages, the exact sequence of eruption cannot be determined when more than one tooth erupts in the time period between two subsequent ages shown on the chart.)

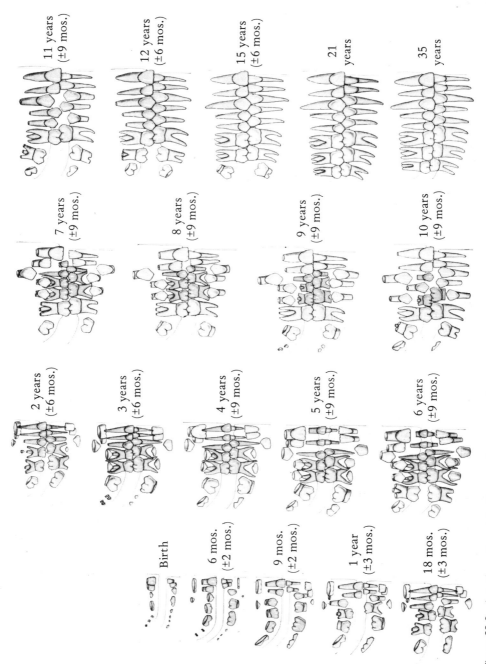

Figure 23-3 Age of eruption of deciduous and permanent dentition.

3. Using the diagram of tooth eruption, write out the order of eruption of the permanent dentition. Uppercase letters are used to refer to the permanent dentition, with I for incisor, C for canine, P for premolar, and M for molar. (See note for problem 2.)

4. The following are lists of teeth present in two skulls. Give the approximate age of each skull.

Skull A: $i^1 i^2 c^1 m^1 m^2 M^1 / i_1 i_2 c_1 m_1 m_2 M_1$

Skull B: $I^1 I^2 c^1 P^1 m^1 M^1 / I_1 I_2 C_1 P_1 m_1 M_1$

ANSWERS

1. A: About 18 to 21 years old

   B: About 15 to 18 years old

   C: About 15.5 to 18.5 years old

2. (The following sequence cannot be entirely deduced from the chart, since the chart does not show all ages.) $i_1 i^1 i_2 i^2 m_1 m^1 c_1^1 m_2^2$

3. See note for answer 2. $M_1^1 I_1^1 I_2 I^2 P_1^1 C_1 P_2^2 C^2 M_2^2 M_3^3$

4. Skull A: About 6 years $\pm$ 9 months

   Skull B: About 10 years $\pm$ 9 months

SUGGESTED READINGS

Kelso, J., and G. Ewing. *Introduction to Physical Anthropology Laboratory Manual.* Boulder, Colo.: Pruett Press, 1962. See laboratory unit 13.

Krogman, W. M. *The Human Skeleton in Forensic Medicine.* Springfield, Ill.: Charles C Thomas, 1962.

Swedlund, A. C., and W. D. Wade. *Laboratory Methods in Physical Anthropology.* Prescott, Ariz.: Prescott College Press, 1972. See supplement 3.

Exercise 24

Folk Taxonomy

All peoples classify the world around them. When such classifications are based on cultural conventions, they are called *folk taxonomies*. Problem 1 shows how such folk taxonomies differ from scientific classifications which are based upon empirical observations. We shall then study folk taxonomies of human variation.

PROBLEM

The world around us is filled with a great variety of animal forms. Biologists divide animals into a series of major categories called *phyla*. Each phylum represents a basic body plan. In this problem you are given ten animals which belong to three distinct phyla. Assuming you have not learned this in a biology course, how would you classify these ten animals into three distinct groups? What criteria would you use in defining each group? After you have completed your classification, compare yours with the scientific classification given below. How do they differ?

Animals   Clam, cockroach, lobster, octopus, sea urchin, shrimp, snail, spider, starfish, wasp.

Your group 1: _____

Criteria used in defining group 1: _____

Your group 2: ————————————————————————————————

Criteria used in defining group 2: ————————————————————————

——

Your group 3: ————————————————————————————————

Criteria used in defining group 3: ————————————————————————

——

ANSWER

The phylum Mollusca contains the clam, octopus, and snail. The mollusks are characterized by a body enclosed in a *dorsal* mantle that secretes a shell, although in some forms, like the octopus, the shell is absent. There is also a *ventral* muscular foot.

The phylum Arthropoda contains the cockroach, lobster, shrimp, spider, and wasp. The arthropods are characterized by such features as a hard external skeleton; legs divided into distinct, movable joints; and jaws which open from side to side.

The phylum Echinodermata contains the starfish and sea urchin. Echinoderms are *radially symmetrical;* have hard, limy plates in the skin; and are all marine.

FOLK TAXONOMIES OF HUMAN VARIATION

In today's world people have contact with other people from many parts of the world. Thus the average American sees a wide range of phenotypes and attempts to categorize these phenotypes into folk taxonomies of human variation. However, just as folk taxonomies of animals little resemble scientific taxonomies, folk taxonomies of human variation do not resemble the biological realities of human variation. In fact, the anthropologist finds it extremely difficult, if not impossible, to divide humankind into any specific number of distinct groups on any rational basis.

PROBLEMS

1. The purpose of this problem is to discover how the American population categorizes human variation. Go to a public area, such as a market or shopping center, or even your own campus, stop a number of individuals, and ask them the same question: How many "races" are there? What are their names? Here we are using the term "race" as a folk taxonomic category and not as a biological term. Also indicate the subjects' sex, age, and "race" as they themselves see it. Record the data on the chart on page 161.

2. After completing the survey, answer the following questions:
    a. What is the average number of "races" specified by your informants? What is the least and greatest number given?
    b. What particular taxonomy was given most frequently? List the different taxonomies and their relative frequencies. For example, note the number who use the familiar threefold classification of Caucasoid, Negroid, and Mongoloid; the number who use color terms such as white, brown, yellow, black, and red; and the number who use ethnic or national terms such as Jew or Irish. What appears to be the rationale behind the various criteria used?
    c. If the people you talk to are of differing ethnic categories themselves, do these different categories of people consistently respond differently?
    d. Why does the division of humankind into three, five, ten, a hundred, or any finite number of categories make little biological sense? Why do these types of categorizations not help us to explain human biological variation?

SUGGESTED READINGS

Molnar, S. *Race, Types, and Ethnic Groups.* Englewood Cliffs, N.J.: Prentice-Hall, 1975.

Pitt-Rivers, J. "The Color of Race," in J. P. Spradley and D. W. McCurdy (eds.), *Conformity and Conflict: Readings in Cultural Anthropology.* Boston: Little, Brown, 1971.

Name _____ Class _____ Date _____

American Folk Taxonomies of "Race"

Sex	Age	"Race"	No. of Groups	Names of Groups

Exercise 25

Taxonomy

Taxonomy is the study of classification, and classification is the first step in any scientific investigation. The problem of classifying data is more difficult than it may appear at first. Consider the following example:

An archaeologist has excavated a site and has found 100 arrowheads. These objects differ in terms of size, shape, material from which they were manufactured, weight, color, function, etc. In addition, no two are exactly alike.

Each characteristic, such as color or presence of a side notch, represents an *attribute*. Each arrowhead is characterized by a large number of such attributes, and each attribute can become the basis for a system of classification. Therefore, it is possible to classify these objects on the basis of size, creating arbitrary groups: for example, those under 1 inch, those between 1 and 2 inches, and those over 2 inches. The same can be done with color or material. The main problem of the archaeologist is to choose those attributes which are most significant to the problem at hand. The details of archaeological classification do not concern us here, but the same types of problems are involved in animal classification.

PROBLEM

Twenty-five household objects are to be classified. Do not read the discussion that follows the list until you have completed the exercise.

Group these objects into any number of categories. Although it is legitimate to have a category of one, for this exercise each category should contain a minimum of two objects. If four or fewer groups are created, divide them into subgroups. If more than ten are created, combine them into larger groupings. When finished, read the discussion.

Objects

1. Key	10. Piece of cloth	19. Bracelet
2. Apple	11. Pencil	20. Paper clip
3. Tin can	12. Ball	21. Spoon
4. Spool of thread	13. Penny	22. Book
5. Block	14. Nail	23. Padlock
6. Index card	15. Paper cup	24. Playing card
7. Screwdriver	16. Rubber band	25. Bar of soap
8. Leaf	17. Flower	
9. Dice	18. Knife	

DISCUSSION

After you have completed the exercise, try it out on others and record and compare the results. What attributes are used as the basis of classification? One classification might be based upon material: metal (key), wood (block), paper (paper cup), etc. Another classification could be based on function: office equipment (paper clip), kitchen utensils (spoon), toys (ball), tools (screwdriver), etc.[1] Shape or color also can be used. Note the different classifications that result. Also note that not all objects fit neatly into a single category. Some objects must be forced into a category, since the exercise does not allow for a category of one. Which objects present problems, and why?

PROBLEM

The problem of classification can be seen in another example, that of library classification of books. Compare the Dewey Decimal System to the Library of Congress System. How do they differ in terms of the criteria used? Give some examples of subjects which would be placed in different categories, depending on the system used. Try to devise a system of classification that is different from either of these.

[1]Of course, this is easy, since we are aware of the functions of these objects because we use them. Identification of function becomes a major problem when foreign objects or archaeological artifacts are used.

Exercise 25

Exercise 26

Chordate Structure

The basic structure of the *chordates* is best seen in *Amphioxus,* a small marine *nonvertebrate* chordate. While generally fishlike in external appearance, it lacks the paired fins, jaws, and vertebral column of the fish. But *Amphioxus* does possess a very well-developed *notochord,* which serves to stiffen the body. Above the notochord (dorsal to the notochord) runs the *nerve cord.* Along the side of the animal are several dozen *gill slits,* which are used not only for breathing but also for food collecting. Small, hairlike projections around the jawless mouth create currents whereby water containing food particles passes into the mouth and out the gills as the animal stays partly submerged in the mud. The food particles adhere to the sticky material found in the "throat," where other hairlike structures move the food back into the intestines.

PROBLEM

To illustrate this basic structure, consider the following two photographs, showing *Amphioxus* as seen through the microscope. Figure 26-1 is a small specimen which has been stained so that the internal features can be seen. Figure 26-2 is a cross section taken perpendicular to the notochord. The important features are indicated by the letters. From the above description, identify the indicated features.

ANSWERS

(A) Notochord; (B) nerve cord; (C) gill slits.

SUGGESTED READING

Romer, A. S. *The Vertebrate Story,* rev. ed. Chicago: Univ. of Chicago Press, 1971.

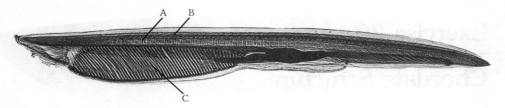

Figure 26-1 *Amphioxus:* whole mount.

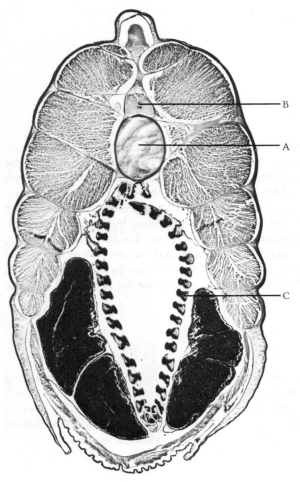

Figure 26-2 *Amphioxus:* cross section.

(A) _____ *(B)* _____ *(C)* _____

Exercise 27

The Mammals

A good way to study the *mammals* is to compare a typical mammal with a typical *reptile*. It is, of course, impossible to provide living animals in a workbook, but Figure 27-1 shows photographs of a living mammal (cheetah) and a reptile (lizard). In addition, you can perhaps observe mammals and reptiles in a pet store or zoo, or even use pets. The other problems call for skeletal material which is presented in photographs.

PROBLEMS

Compare a live mammal, such as a dog, cat, hamster, or mouse, with a live reptile, such as a lizard, turtle, or snake.

1. What differences exist in body posture, i.e., the position of the legs with respect to the body? Compare the methods of locomotion if possible.

2. Locate the external ear of the two forms. How do they differ?

Figure 27-1a A living mammal (cheetah).

3. What differences exist in outside covering?

4. Compare each animal's apparent awareness of its environment. Does it notice your movements? What senses seem to predominate in noting your activities?[1]

[1]Live animals are needed for questions 4 and 5. Omit if not available.

Exercise 27

Figure 27-1b Living reptiles (*Anolis*).

5. Compare the forms in terms of activity. How does each respond to external stimuli?

PROBLEMS

Figure 27-2 shows photographs of a cat skeleton and a crocodile skeleton.

1. How does the position of the limbs with respect to the body differ in the two forms?

Figure 27-2a   Mammalian skeleton (cat).

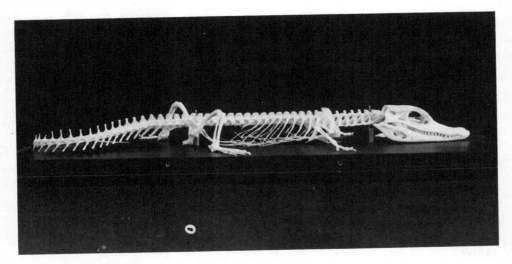

Figure 27-2b   Reptilian skeleton (crocodile).

2. How does the skull attach to the spine?

3. What is the relative length of the limbs as compared to the spine?

4. What other skeletal differences do you observe? (*Note:* One difference you cannot observe is the difference in the middle ear bones. Reptiles have only one middle ear bone, while mammals have three.)

PROBLEMS

Figure 27-3 shows photographs of the skull of a cat and a crocodile.

1. Are there any ridges of bone on the skull?

2. How does the lower jaw articulate with the skull?

3. Describe the structure of the teeth. How do they differ?

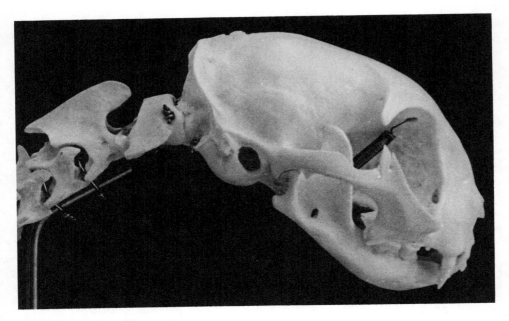

Figure 27-3a Mammalian skull (cat).

Figure 27-3b Reptilian skull (crocodile).

Exercise 28

Observations of Living Primates

The best way to illustrate *primate* characteristics is to spend some time observing primates at a zoo. If a zoo is not convenient, attempt to observe a primate in a pet store. You might want to do this exercise along with Exercises 29 and 30, which also require a trip to the zoo.

PROBLEMS

First, to illustrate the basic features of the primate complex, locate an *Old World monkey,* preferably one of the more arboreal forms, such as the guenons or mangabeys.

1. Note the general proportions of the body, especially the length of the limbs relative to the length of the body. What is the advantage of long limbs to an arboreal form? As the animal moves around, note the position of the arms and the degree of movement in the shoulder.

2. Observe the nails on the digits as well as the position of the thumb with respect to the other fingers. How does the monkey use its hand in locomotion? In feeding? In picking up objects?

3. What different methods does the animal use in moving around in its cage?

4. Note the structure of the face. What is the basic shape of the head? To what degree do the nose and jaw project from the face? What is the position of the eyes? What senses does the animal appear to be using when picking up objects or simply examining the observer?

5. After completing these basic observations, examine the forms listed below.

6. Select an example of a species of each of the following: prosimian, New World monkey, Old World monkey, ape, and a human. Then complete the chart on page 177 comparing these five animals.

The following are brief descriptions of primates likely to be seen in a zoo.

Lemur The ring-tailed lemur is the only *prosimian* which is frequently found on display. This animal is *diurnal,* spends some time on the ground, and lives in social groups, quite unlike most prosimians. Note the position of the eyes and the elaboration of the snout. The sense of smell plays an important role in lemur activity. In fact, if the animal is disturbed, it will sometimes mark out its territory by rubbing the anal region up and down the bars of the cage, a behavior known as *scent-marking.* Note that the legs are longer than the arms, an adaptation for leaping. The hand is basically primatelike, but the thumb is in no way opposable. Note the presence of nails on all digits except the second toe. In grooming, most primates use their hands, but the lemur will use its *dental comb.* The lemurs are highly social and at rest come into very close contact with one another.

Marmoset   The marmosets are *New World monkeys* and are the smallest of all the monkeys. They do not show all primate tendencies. Like many prosimians, they are not capable of facial expression. They possess clawlike nails. Marmosets do not perform as well as other monkeys on psychological tests. There are many forms of marmosets, the smallest being the pygmy marmoset.

Squirrel Monkey   The squirrel monkey is perhaps the best known of the New World monkeys which lack a prehensile tail. These are rather small animals. Note the *platyrrhine nose,* the lack of the opposable thumb, and the lack of the *ischial callosities* and *sexual skin* found in many of the Old World forms.

Spider Monkey   The spider monkey is one of the most popular New World zoo monkeys but you may see other examples of monkeys with *prehensile tails,* such as the woolly monkeys. The prehensile tail of this form is naked on the underside, where the animal is able to feel. The tail is used in locomotion, for suspension, and for picking up objects. Note the absence of a thumb.

Macaques   The macaques are semiterrestrial forms from Asia; the rhesus macaque of India is the common laboratory monkey. The Japanese macaque is the only temperate-dwelling nonhuman primate (except for the Gibraltar macaque of Europe) and is able to survive the winter snows. Note the *catarrhine* nose and the well-developed thumb. Some of the macaques have little or no tail.

Baboons   The several species of baboons are the most terrestrial of the monkeys. The baboons inhabit the grasslands of Africa, and one species even ranges in a semi-desert area. These forms show a marked *sexual dimorphism,* that is, differences in size and structure between the sexes. The young are born a dark color but gradually change to the adult color after several months. Note the ischial callosities and sexual skin. In the *estrus* female the sexual skin becomes greatly swollen.

Gibbon   The gibbon is one of the *lesser apes.* Note the absence of the tail and the short, compact trunk, which contrasts with the extremely long arms and fingers. This form is noted for its pattern of locomotion, *brachiation,* whereby the animal hangs from a branch and moves hand over hand.

Orangutan   The *great apes* include the orangutan, chimpanzees, and gorilla. The orangutan provides a good example of sexual dimorphism. The adult male is about twice as large as the adult female. The male of the Borneo subspecies is also characterized by flanges about the face. The hair may appear to be poorly groomed, but that is merely the way it grows. Orangutans appear slow and deliberate in their movements, but they can move fast if necessary. They are basically arboreal in habit in the wild.

Gorilla   The gorilla normally seen in captivity is the lowland gorilla of West Africa. The adults show some sexual dimorphism, and the older adult males develop gray fur along their back, hence the name "silver-backed males." Note the typical musty odor.

SUGGESTED READINGS

Eimerl, S., and I. DeVore. *The Primates.* New York: Time-Life Books, 1965.

Napier, J. R., and P. H. Napier. *A Handbook of Living Primates.* New York: Academic, 1967.

Schultz, A. H. *The Life of Primates.* New York: Universe Books, 1969.

Features	Prosimian	NW Monkey	OW Monkey	Ape	Human
Name of species					
Body size					
Length of tail as proportion of body length					
Relative length of forelimb and hindlimb					
Structure of hand; nails; degree of opposability					
Notes on head: nose, ears, eyes, and dentition					
Coloration					
Nature and degree of sexual dimorphism					
Movements and locomotion					

Exercise 29

An Exercise in Observing Primate Behavior

The behavior of primates in captivity may differ markedly from behavior in natural habitats. Yet comparative studies of captive and wild populations have shown that under good captive conditions the qualitative aspects of behavior differ little from those in the wild. In captivity, however, social interaction is apt to be more frequent and more intense. Under unsatisfactory conditions in captivity, such as little space, inadequate diet, and lack of companionship, behavior can be quite unnatural.

We can use observations of zoo populations to illustrate many aspects of primate behavior. In this exercise, locate and observe a group of primates. Observation of behavioral patterns requires familiarity with the individuals of the group, and so it is better to study one group intensively for several hours than to study a number of groups, each for a short period of time.

The study is divided into three sections. Section A is a preliminary study designed to familiarize you with the group. Section B is a short quantitative study. Section C deals with observations of behavior in general. It is suggested that this exercise be done in conjunction with the study of primate locomotion in Exercise 30.

SECTION A

Note the following information:

1. Name of zoo

2. Species being studied (common and scientific name)

3. Census
   a. Number of animals
   b. Classification of animals by sex and age. (Sex may be difficult to determine in young animals; age may be given in terms of age categories: infant, juvenile, subadult, adult.)
4. Description of environment (size, shape, features)
5. Major locomotor habits
6. Methods of feeding and drinking, including notes on diet
7. Methods of holding and manipulating objects; examples of tool use
8. Notes on individual animals from zoo personnel
9. Notes on naturalistic behavior from literature

SECTION B

Choose one animal as your subject. List the other animals in the cage on the score sheet. Follow the activities of the chosen animal and at thirty-second intervals record which other animal or animals the subject is interacting with at that moment, and the general nature of the interaction (e.g., grooming, carrying, mounting, threatening). Follow the same animal for at least ten minutes. Repeat for two or three other animals. Repeat for the same animals after a period of time or the next day.

This exercise will help you to recognize individuals and be aware of their activity. It will also give you an idea of the intensity of social interactions during the period of time they were observed.

SECTION C

After you have become familiar with the group and have completed the above studies, proceed to observe the same group of primates over a period of one hour. During this time, note the exact time at approximately five-minute intervals. Write down your observations. Be sure to write down only what you actually see, and be certain to identify the individuals involved. These are your field notes, so do not attempt any interpretation at this time.

After your study is complete, review your field notes and see if any generalizations can be made. Then write a one- or two-page paper describing the general behavior of your particular group, using your field notes to support your generalizations and interpretations. The following example can be used as a model.

From Field Notes (2:15 P.M.): Male A approaches male B, who is sitting next to the feeding dish. As male A approaches within 25 feet, male B looks up at male A repeatedly. When male A is within 15 feet of male B, male B moves away to the back of the cage, where he immediately begins to groom female A. Male A looks at male B, slaps the ground, and then settles down to eat.

(2:35 P.M.): Male A is sitting in center of cage. As male B moves across the cage from left to right, male A watches. When male B is within 20 feet of male A, male A displays his canines. Male B runs to right of cage.

(2:55 P.M.): Male B is sitting on a boulder located in the left background of the cage. Male A approaches. When male A is within 15 feet of the boulder, male B quickly leaves and moves to the right side of the cage. Male A then leaps on the top of the boulder and sits down.

Generalizations Whenever male A approaches male B, the latter moves out of the way. Male A can threaten male B and male B will not return the threat. Male B was never observed to threaten male A.

Interpretation A *dominance hierarchy* exists among the adult males of this group. Male A is dominant with respect to male B, as seen by displacement and threat gestures.

The following are some suggestions as to the types of behavioral patterns you might observe.

1. The males may be ranked in a dominance hierarchy. The males will generally be dominant to the females. The relative position in the dominance system is expressed in several ways. Chief among these are: *displacement*, where the subordinate animal gives way to the dominant one; *mounting*, where the dominant animal mounts the subordinate one; and preferred choice of food, sitting place, and estrus females. Females with infants will rank quite high among the females and will be the center of grooming activity.

2. Close social bonds are often expressed in terms of grooming. *Grooming* is usually carried on by females. Females usually groom adult males only as a part of courtship. Note the intensity of grooming activity and the identification of the participants. Is there a relationship between grooming activity and dominance?

3. Note the intensely close relationship between a mother and a young infant. The infant will rarely leave its mother and will be carried on her belly or back when the mother travels. Is the infant passed among the troop and, if so, to whom? Note how the adult males tolerate the presence of an infant. Note also the presence of play groups, their membership, and the types of play behavior.

4. Much primate social interaction is expressed in terms of gesture and vocalization. Note the identity (age, sex, and dominance rank) of the animals involved in the act of communication, and describe in detail the behavior involved. Be careful not to read human qualities into an expression. A yawn by a baboon, for example, does not necessarily indicate boredom but is usually a threat gesture.

5. You may observe sexual behavior. In some forms, the sexual skin of the female enlarges and/or changes color. In captivity, however, the sexual skin may remain large after the completion of estrus if there are no sexually mature males in the cage. The female is often the initiator of sexual activity.

An Exercise in Observing Primate Behavior

SUGGESTED READINGS

Bramblett, C. A. *Patterns of Primate Behavior*. Palo Alto, Calif.: Mayfield, 1976.

DeVore, I. (ed.). *Primate Behavior: Field Studies of Monkeys and Apes*. New York: Holt, 1965.

Dolhinow, P. (ed.). *Primate Patterns*. New York: Holt, 1972.

Jolly, A. *The Evolution of Primate Behavior*. New York: Macmillan, 1972.

Kummer, H. *Primate Societies*. Chicago: Aldine-Atherton, 1971.

Rowell, T. *The Social Behaviour of Monkeys*. Baltimore: Penguin, 1972.

Name _____ Class _____ Date _____

Species _____ Zoo _____

Subject _____

List Members of Group Other Than Subject	Nature of Interaction

Name _____ Class _____ Date _____

Species _____ Zoo _____

Subject _____

List Members of Group Other Than Subject	Nature of Interaction

184

Name _____ Class _____ Date _____

Species _____ Zoo _____

Subject _____

List Members of Group Other Than Subject	Nature of Interaction

Name ———————————— Class ——————— Date ———————

Species ———————————— Zoo ————————————

Subject ————————————————————

List Members of Group Other Than Subject	Nature of Interaction

Exercise 30

Primate Locomotion

A very important area of primate behavior is the study of primate locomotion. Primates show a great variety of locomotion patterns. Some patterns involve all four limbs, such as quadrupedal walking and running. These behaviors may take place on the ground or along a branch, and the primate may walk or run with the hands palm down or on the knuckles of the hand, as is the case with the chimpanzees and gorillas. Many primates will also walk bipedally—that is, on the legs alone—and in humans this has become a specialized means of locomotion. In the trees primates show a variety of locomotor patterns in addition to arboreal quadrupedalism. These include leaping, swinging, and brachiation. The latter pattern involves suspension by the arms from a branch and a hand-over-hand progression on a branch. Some New World monkeys possess prehensile tails, which make possible a type of locomotion known as semibrachiation. Here the animal suspends itself under a branch by its tail alone, or by its tail and one or both arms.

In addition to these locomotion behaviors, primates spend a great deal of time simply sitting or standing or lying down in a variety of positions.

PROBLEMS

1. Select a particular species of primate and choose a specific animal for study. Using the form on page 189, conduct a quantitative study of that animal's locomotor behavior. Have another person mark off ten-second intervals. At each ten-second interval, determine the pattern of locomotion seen in that animal at that particular time. Follow the same animal for ten minutes, or sixty determinations. Be sure to record the age and sex and species of the animal under study.

2. Using the second form, repeat the same study with the same animal at a different time of day, a different animal of the same species, or a member of another species.

Napier and Napier define four general categories of locomotor behavior: *vertical clinging and leaping, quadrupedalism, brachiation,* and *bipedalism.* [1] The classification of a specific locomotor pattern is difficult, since it may not fit neatly into one category, and any given species will show a great variety of patterns.

In vertical clinging and leaping the animal rests on a branch, clinging to that branch in a vertical position. It then leaps, landing vertically on a second branch (e.g., indri, tarsier). In quadrupedalism the animal moves on all fours with its body held parallel to the ground. There are several forms of quadrupedalism. In the *slow-climbing type* the animal moves slowly and cautiously along the branch (e.g., slender loris). In *branch running and walking* the animal climbs, jumps, and leaps among the branches and walks and runs along the branches on all fours (e.g., lemur, guenon, langur). *Ground running and walking* is similar, except that it takes place on a hard, flat surface (e.g., baboon). In *New World semibrachiation* [2] the animal uses its hands and prehensile tail to suspend and propel the body (e.g., spider monkey). In *Old World semibrachiation* we observe leaping with the arms extended outward to grasp a branch (e.g., Colobus monkey).

In *true brachiation* the body is suspended from a branch by the arms and moves swinging the arms hand over hand (e.g., gibbon). In *modified brachiation* the hind limbs are used a great deal to support the body (e.g., orangutan). Although they are classed as modified brachiators by the Napiers, it is perhaps better to view the chimpanzee and the gorilla as *knuckle walkers.* Although several primates can locomote bipedally over short distances, the Napiers use the term *bipedalism* to refer to the heel-toe stride found only in humans.

PROBLEM

After completing your observational study, classify the species under study into one of the Napier categories. What difficulties do you encounter?

Note that this study is very limited in time. Since frequencies of various locomotor patterns may vary from hour to hour or from day to day, do not make generalizations from a limited study. The purpose of this exercise is not to develop such generalizations but to familiarize you with locomotor behavior among primates.

SUGGESTED READING

Napier, J. R., and P. H. Napier. *A Handbook of the Living Primates.* New York: Academic, 1967.

[1] J. R. Napier and P. H. Napier, *A Handbook of the Living Primates.* (New York: Academic, 1967), pp. 385–391.

[2] Although the term *semibrachiation* is used, this is still a form of quadrupedalism.

Name _____ Class _____ Date _____

Species _____ Sex _____ Age _____

Locomotor or Posture Pattern	Number of Times Observed
Sitting	
Standing on all fours	
Standing on two legs	
Standing on two legs with support	
Lying on front	
Lying on side	
Lying on back	
Ground walking on palms	
Ground walking on knuckles	
Ground running on knuckles	
Branch walking	
Branch running	
Leaping	
Swinging	
Brachiation	
Suspended by tail	
Suspended by tail and one or both arms	

Name _____ Class _____ Date _____

Species _____ Sex _____ Age _____

Locomotor or Posture Pattern	Number of Times Observed
Sitting	
Standing on all fours	
Standing on two legs	
Standing on two legs with support	
Lying on front	
Lying on side	
Lying on back	
Ground walking on palms	
Ground walking on knuckles	
Ground running on knuckles	
Branch walking	
Branch running	
Leaping	
Swinging	
Brachiation	
Suspended by tail	
Suspended by tail and one or both arms	

Exercise 31

Comparative Anatomy of the Primate Skeleton

The primates in general have maintained great flexibility in locomotor patterns and the skeleton has remained quite generalized, similar to the fossils of the earliest mammals, especially in comparison to other types of mammals such as a cat, horse, or giraffe. Anatomical differences among primates are, in part, related to differences in locomotor patterns.

The ancestral primate had short limbs and a long vertebral column. An adaptive trend in primate evolution has been the lengthening of both forelimbs and hindlimbs and a shortening of the vertebral column. In fact, among modern primates, except some lorises and marmosets, the limbs are longer than the vertebral column, a condition which allows a longer stride. The Napiers make these correlations:

Length of Limbs Relative to Length of Trunk	Habitat	Locomotor Habit
Short limbs	Arboreal	Adaptation for quadrupedal gait
Long limbs	Ground-living	Adaptation for quadrupedal gait
Long forelimbs	Arboreal	Adaptation for brachiation
Long hindlimbs	Arboreal	Adaptation for vertical clinging and leaping

Source: J. R. Napier and P. H. Napier, *A Handbook of the Living Primates* (New York: Academic, 1967).

While the basic trend in primate evolution has been toward a lengthening of the forelimbs and hindlimbs, there is great variability in the ratio between arm and leg lengths which can also be correlated with locomotor pattern. This can be seen in the *intermembral index:*

$$\frac{\text{Humerus} + \text{radius length}}{\text{Femur} + \text{tibia length}} \times 100$$

The three basic patterns of the intermembral index are:

Intermembral index 50–80   Vertical clinging and leaping; bipedalism
Intermembral index 80–100   Quadrupedalism
Intermembral index 100–150   Brachiation

PROBLEMS

1.   The following are photographs of a cat skeleton and a monkey skeleton (rhesus macaque). Compare the two skeletons. Note the relative length of the limbs to the trunk and the position of the skull on the spine.

2.   Calculate the intermembral indices from the photographs (beginning on page 196) of the following skeletons: tarsier (vertical clinging and leaping), squirrel monkey (quadrupedalism), rhesus macaque (quadrupedalism), chimpanzee (knuckle walking), and human (bipedalism). Using a ruler, measure the bones in the photographs. Calculate the intermembral indices and record them on the chart on page 201. How do the indices relate to locomotor patterns?

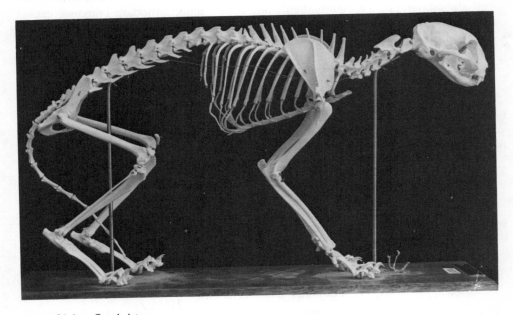

Figure 31-1a   Cat skeleton.

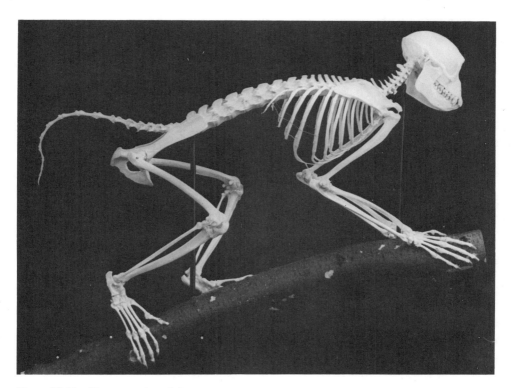

Figure 31-1b Rhesus monkey skeleton.

ANSWERS

2. Since these measurements are made on photographs, they are not precise, and your indices may vary slightly from those given below. It should be realized that within a given species there is a range of variation of all measurements and indices and the skeletons shown here represent a single sample from the population. Also, the intermembral index of the infant chimpanzee differs somewhat from that of an adult since the relative proportions of limbs do change with age.

Primate	Intermembral Index from Photo Specimen	Major Locomotor Pattern
Tarsier	51	Vertical clinging and leaping
Squirrel monkey	86	Quadrupedalism
Rhesus monkey	91	Quadrupedalism
Chimpanzee	120	Knuckle walking
Human	80	Bipedalism

SUGGESTED READING

LeGros Clark, W. E. *The Antecedents of Man.* Edinburgh: Edinburgh Univ. Press, 1959.

Comparative Anatomy of the Primate Skeleton

Figure 31-2a Skeleton of a tarsier.

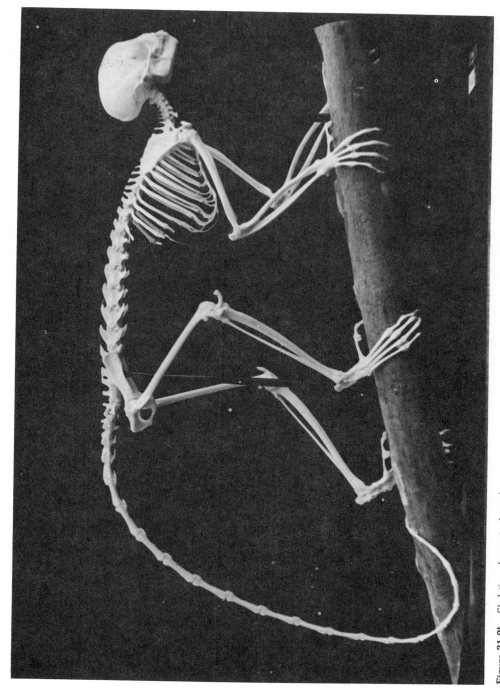

Figure 31-2b Skeleton of a squirrel monkey.

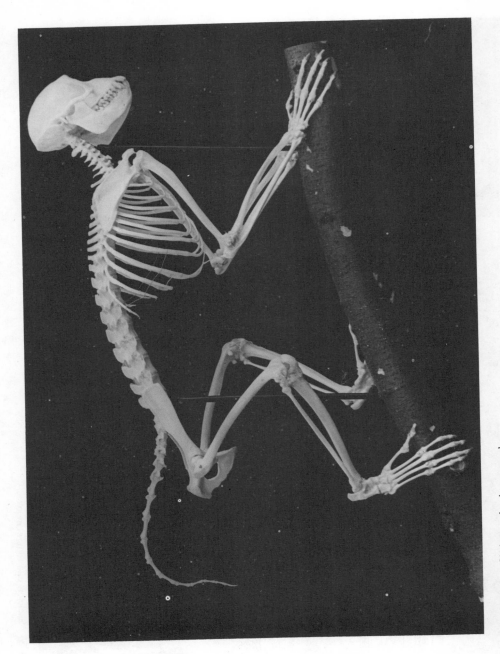

Figure 31-2c   Skeleton of a rhesus monkey.

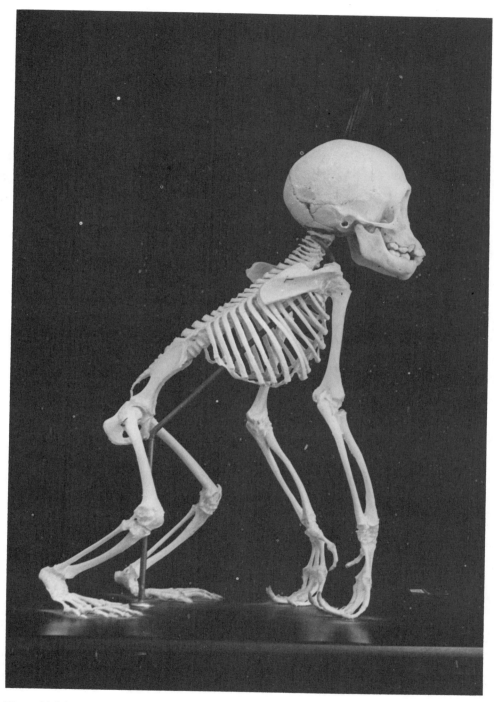

Figure 31-2d Skeleton of an infant chimpanzee.

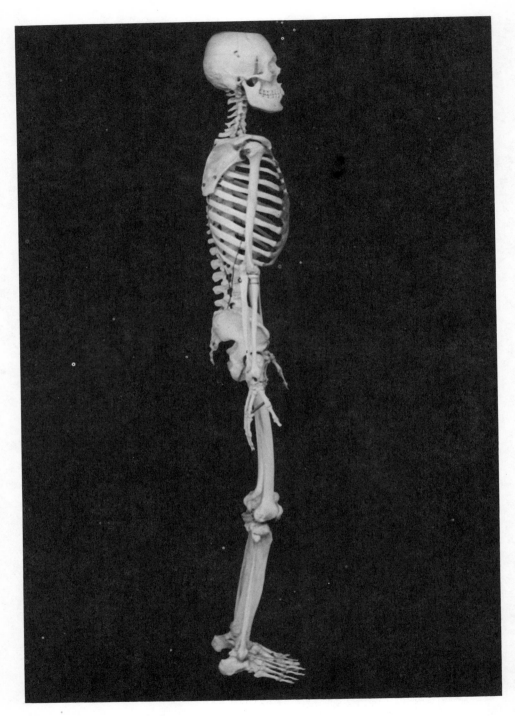

Figure 31-2e Skeleton of a human.

Primate	Length of Humerus	Length of Radius	Length of Femur	Length of Tibia	Intermembral Index
Tarsier					
Squirrel monkey					
Rhesus monkey					
Chimpanzee					
Human					

Exercise 32

Comparative Anatomy of the Primate Skull

W. E. LeGros Clark lists the following trends in primate evolution which can be seen in the skull:[1]

1. The progressive enlargement of the brain case, which becomes more globular in shape and often lacks the prominent bony crests found in many other mammals

2. The enclosure of the orbit by a complete bony ring and, in higher primates, the formation of a bony wall shutting it off behind

3. The gradual rotation forward of the orbits until their openings face directly forward

4. The narrowing of the bony arch to the cheek (zygomatic arch)

5. The recession of the snout, and the retraction of the face to a position below rather than in front of the cranium

6. The shrinkage of the bony apparatus of the nose

7. The progressive shifting of the foramen magnum from the back end of the skull to its underside, so that it opens downward instead of more or less backward

PROBLEMS

1. Compare a cat and a monkey skull (Figure 32-1) in light of the trends mentioned above.

[1]W. E. LeGros Clark, *History of the Primates,* 5th ed. (Chicago: Univ. of Chicago Press, 1965), p. 23.

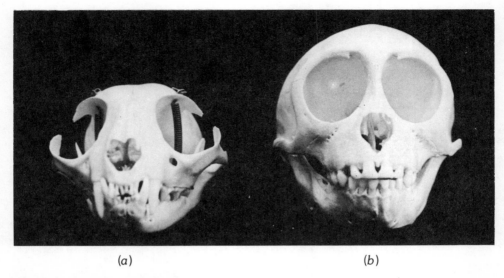

Figure 32-1 Skulls of (a) a cat and (b) a monkey.

2. Examine a prosimian skull and compare it with a monkey skull (Figure 32-2). What major differences can you see?

3. Some higher primates possess a forward, protruding lower portion of the face, which is a *dental muzzle* rather than an *olfactory muzzle*. Compare the skull of a baboon with that of a rhesus monkey (Figure 32-3).

(a)

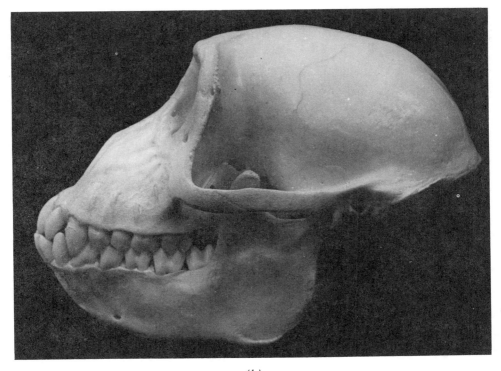

(b)

Figure 32-2 Skulls of (a) a prosimian (slender loris) and (b) a rhesus monkey.

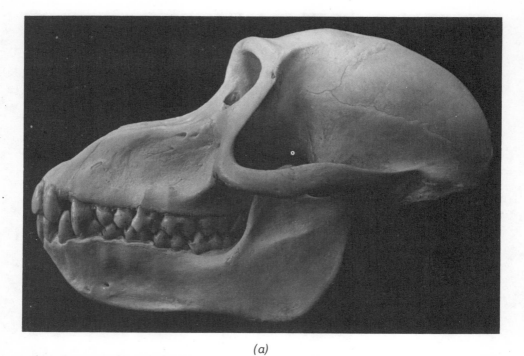

(a)

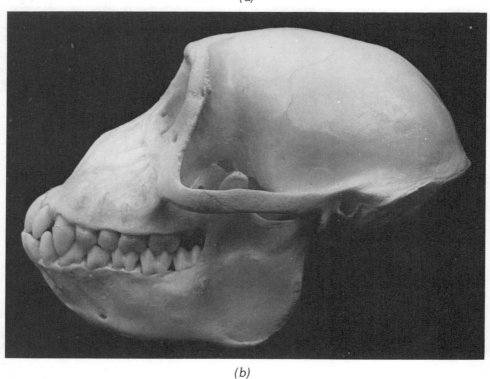

(b)

Figure 32-3 Skulls of (*a*) a baboon and (*b*) a rhesus monkey.

4. The surface of the skull serves as a place for the attachment of muscles. When the muscles are large and the surface area of the skull is small, special crests develop. In an animal with a heavy jaw but a small brain case, a special crest, the *sagittal crest,* develops along the top of the skull cap for the attachment of the *temporalis muscle.* The *nuchal crest,* at the base of the occipital bone at the back of the skull, is for the attachment of the muscles which serve to hold the skull upright on the spine. The brow ridge is also a manifestation of a heavy jaw. Compare these features on the skulls of the apes.

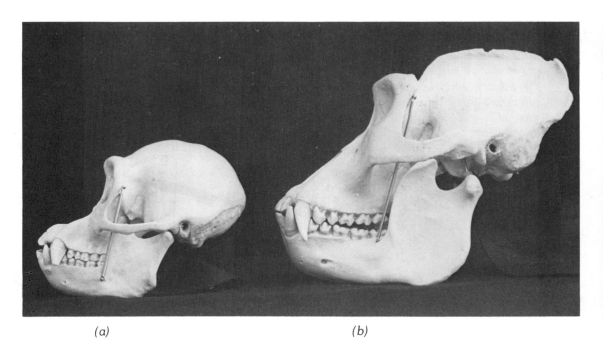

(a) *(b)*

Figure 32-4 Skulls of (a) a chimpanzee and (b) a gorilla.

Comparative Anatomy of the Primate Skull

Exercise 33

Comparative Anatomy of Primate Dentition

Like all mammals, the primates are characterized by *heterodonty,* the regional differentiation of teeth. One of the basic trends in the evolution of primate dentition has been a reduction in the number of teeth from the ancestral forty-four to between thirty-two and thirty-six. A fairly simple *cusp pattern* has been retained.

The number and types of teeth are indicated by the *dental formula.* The ancestral mammalian dental formula is $\frac{3.1.4.3}{3.1.4.3}$; that is, in one half of the upper jaw we find three *incisors,* one *canine,* four *premolars,* and three *molars,* and in one half of the lower jaw we find the same.

Most living primates have lost one incisor in the upper and lower jaw. The premolars have been reduced from four to three in prosimians and New World monkeys, and to two in the Old World monkeys, apes, and humans. Three molars have been retained except for a tendency for the reduction or loss of the third molar in many species, including humans.

PROBLEMS
1. Determine the dental formulas for the mandibles shown in Figure 33-1.

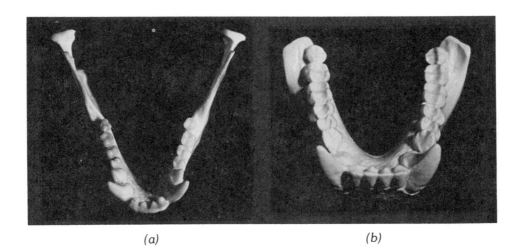

(a) (b)

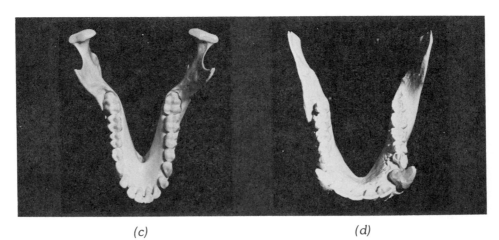

(c) (d)

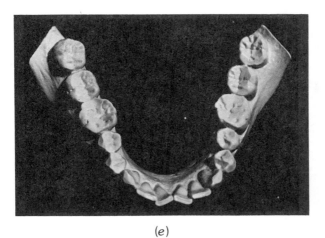

(e)

Figure 33-1 Mandibles:
(a) marmoset, (b) squirrel monkey,
(c) rhesus monkey, (d) chimpanzee,
(e) human.

Comparative Anatomy of Primate Dentition

Primate	Dental Formula
Marmoset	
Squirrel monkey	
Rhesus monkey	
Chimpanzee	
Human	

2. Note the *dental comb* in the slender loris (see Figure 33-2). This structure consists of the elongated lower incisors and canines projecting forward horizontally. The comb is used primarily for grooming.

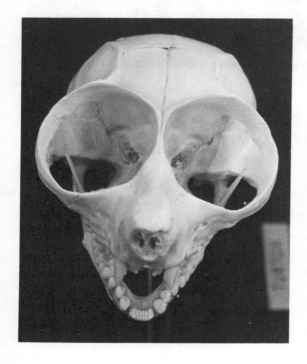

Figure 33-2 Skull of the slender loris.

3. Compare the upper and lower jaws of a human with those of the chimpanzee. Make a list of all observed differences and similarities. (See Figure 33-1*d* and *e* for lower jaws.)

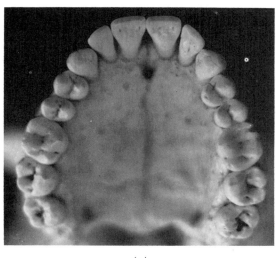

(a)

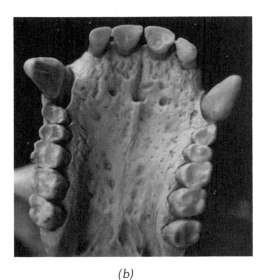

(b)

Figure 33-3 Upper jaw: (*a*) human, (*b*) chimpanzee.

ANSWERS

1. Marmoset   2.1.3.2/2.1.3.2
    Squirrel monkey   2.1.3.3/2.1.3.3
    Rhesus monkey   2.1.2.3/2.1.2.3
    Chimpanzee   2.1.2.3/2.1.2.3
    Human   2.1.2.3/2.1.2.3

3. Among the similarities which might be noted are the same number and kinds of teeth. Among the differences which might be noted are:

Human	Chimpanzee
No gaps (diastema) in tooth row	Gap (diastema) between incisor and canine
Canine does not project	Projecting canine
Tooth row is roughly a parabolic arch	Premolars and molars arranged in roughly parallel rows

SUGGESTED READING

LeGros Clark, W. E. *History of the Primates,* 5th ed. Chicago: Univ. of Chicago Press, 1965.

Exercise 34

Radiometric Dating

The term *radiometric dating* refers to a series of *absolute dating* techniques based upon the natural decay of radioactive substances. Some materials are composed of unstable *atoms* whose *nuclei* are constantly losing particles. This loss process is termed "radioactive decay." The rate of decay can be measured and serves as a dating method. One of the best-known radiometric dating methods is *radiocarbon dating*, which is based upon the radioactive form of carbon, carbon 14 (C^{14}).

When an atom of nitrogen in the upper atmosphere is bombarded by *cosmic radiation (neutrons)*, an atom of C^{14} (and a *proton*) is formed. This newly formed C^{14} combines with oxygen to form carbon dioxide, which is then incorporated into plants by photosynthesis and into animals ingesting plants or other animals. A living organism is constantly taking in new C^{14}. The amount of C^{14} taken into the body equals the amount of C^{14} lost by radioactive decay. However, when an organism dies, no new C^{14} enters the organism and the C^{14} which is present at the moment of death will disappear through time because of radioactive decay.

PROBLEMS

1. It is impossible to predict when a particular atom of C^{14} will decay. But it is possible to make a statistical statement about the rate of decay of a group of such atoms. The *half-life* of a radioactive substance is the time it takes for one-half of the atoms to decay into new atoms. In the case of C^{14} this is the amount of time it takes for one-half of the C^{14} atoms present to decay into N^{14}. The half-life of C^{14} is approximately 5,730 years. This means that if we started out with a million atoms of C^{14} we would be left with only half a million atoms after 5,730 years had elapsed. An additional 5,730 years would reduce the number of atoms again by half, giving a total of one-fourth of a million atoms after a total of 11,460 years.

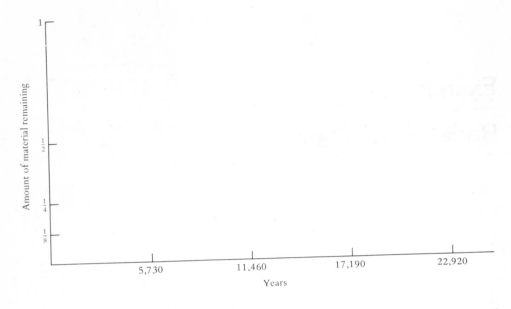

The concept of half-life perhaps can best be illustrated with a graph. On the blank graph above, the vertical axis has been marked off in terms of fractions of the original number of atoms left, while the horizontal axis has been marked off in terms of the half-life of C^{14}. Construct a decay curve by placing a dot where the line from each half-life or multiple of a half-life intersects the line from the vertical axis giving the amount of radioactive material remaining.

2. Once a living organism dies, no additional C^{14} is incorporated into the body, but the C^{14} already present continues to decay. Thus, after 5,730 years, only one-half of the number of original C^{14} atoms remain. To put this another way, the level of radioactivity as measured by a geiger counter will be half of what it would be on a fresh specimen. Thus the method of calculating the absolute date of an organism—or, more precisely, the date at which the organism died—is to compare the amount of radioactivity of a fresh specimen to that of the specimen being dated.

Using the decay chart which you have drawn, calculate the approximate date of the materials listed below. To do this, you simply locate the amount of radioactivity on the vertical axis of your graph and follow that line over to the point where it intersects the curve. At this point drop a line directly downward and read the absolute date (in terms of number of years old) on the horizontal axis.

    a. Three-fourths of the radioactivity of a fresh specimen

    b. Two-thirds of the radioactivity of a fresh specimen

    c. Three-eighths of the radioactivity of a fresh specimen

3. In actual practice, the carbon found in a sample is extracted as a gas and its radioactivity is measured in an elaborate geiger counter. Each time an atom of C^{14} decays, a count is registered on the counter. Although the rate of decay varies somewhat depending on the material being measured (charcoal, wood, bone, shell, etc.), a gram of pure carbon from a contemporary source will register decay on the counter at an average rate of 15.27 counts per minute. The decay of any single atom is a random event, and this figure is an average calculated over an extended period.

Exercise 34

In the laboratory, the absolute dates are calculated not by means of a graph but by a formula:

$$t = \log\frac{I_0}{I} \times \lambda \text{ years}$$

where t = absolute age

I_0 = activity of a contemporary sample, in this case 15.27 counts per minute

I = activity of the sample being dated

λ = decay constant, which is another way of expressing the half-life (the decay constant for C^{14} is 18.5×10^3)

Using the above formula, calculate the absolute date of a piece of charcoal, which gives a rate of decay of 4.20 counts per minute. In order to do this calculation, you will need a table of logarithms or a calculator which gives log.

4. Since the decay rate is a statistical statement, there is a built-in error in all radiocarbon determinations. Thus all radiocarbon dates are given in the following form: 7,000 ± 100 years. The ± 100 years represents the standard deviation for this particular determination. For an explanation of standard deviation see Exercise 15.

The existence of a standard deviation can cause problems in interpretation. For example, two specimens are dated at 8,100 ± 120 and 8,025 ± 110 years, respectively. This means that the most likely dates for the first sample fall between 7,980 and 8,220 years, while for the second sample they fall between 7,915 and 8,135 years. Therefore, the first specimen could actually be younger than the second if, for example, the real dates were 8,025 and 8,100, respectively.

The following is a list of six dates for six objects found in different locations within the same *site*. Place these objects in a probable chronological order as well as you can, based upon their radiocarbon dates.

Object A	2,370 ± 50 years	Object D	2,910 ± 80 years
Object B	2,750 ± 70 years	Object E	2,540 ± 60 years
Object C	2,600 ± 60 years	Object F	2,700 ± 60 years

5. The radiocarbon method of absolute dating is based upon the assumption that the rate of creation of C^{14} in the upper atmosphere has been constant through time. Since it has been demonstrated that cosmic radiation bombardment is not constant, neither is the creation of C^{14}. The radiocarbon dating of material of known date has shown a systematic error. Thus radiocarbon dates calculated by the formula should be thought of as being in terms of *radiocarbon years* rather than *calendar years*. However, we are slowly learning to correct for the error, and thus we should be able to convert radiocarbon years into calendar years by adding or subtracting the appropriate number of years contained in the error. Using Table 34-1, which shows the average deviation of radiocarbon years from calendar dates, convert the ages below into calendar dates. Assume that these radiocarbon dates were calculated in 1950.

    a. 1,625

    b. 2,450

    c. 3,000

    d. 4,225

ANSWERS

3. $t = \log \dfrac{I_0}{I} \times \lambda$ years $t = 0.561 \times 18.5 \times 10^3$ years

                                          $t = 10,371$ years

    $t = \log \dfrac{15.27}{4.20} \times 18.5 \times 10^3$ years

4. There is a definite sequence from older to younger as follows: A, C, B, D. E is older than F, but since the most probable range of dates for E overlaps that of C, and F overlaps that of B and C, the exact placement of E and F in the sequence is not certain from the C^{14} dates alone.

5.   **a.** A.D. 375   **c.** 1150 B.C.
      b. 550 B.C.   **d.** 2825 B.C.

SUGGESTED READINGS

Michael, H. N., and E. K. Ralph (eds.). *Dating Techniques for the Archaeologist.* Cambridge, Mass.: MIT Press, 1971.

Michels, J. W. *Dating Methods in Prehistory.* New York: Seminar Press, 1973.

Watkins, T. (ed.). *Radiocarbon: Calibration and Prehistory.* Edinburgh: Edinburgh Univ. Press, 1975.

Table 34-1 Conversion Table for Radiocarbon Dates

Time Period Represented by Radiocarbon Dates	Average Deviation of C¹⁴ Dates*	Calendar Period Represented by Precisely Dated Tree-Ring Samples	Number of Samples
A.D. 1525 – 1879	+ 50	A.D. 1500–1829 (329 years)	12
A.D. 1250 – 1524	0	A.D. 1250–1499	7
A.D. 975 – 1249	0	A.D. 1000–1249	8
A.D. 700 – 974	− 50	A.D. 750– 999	4
A.D. 450 – 699	− 50	A.D. 500– 749	11
A.D. 200 – 449	− 50	A.D. 250– 499	9
25 B.C. to A.D. 200	− 50	A.D. 1– 249	7
225 B.C. – 26 B.C.	0	249– 1 B.C.	7
450 – 226 B.C.	+ 50	499– 250 B.C.	7
675 – 451 B.C.	+ 50	749– 500 B.C.	7
900 – 676 B.C.	+100	999– 750 B.C.	8
1125 – 901 B.C.	+100	1249–1000 B.C.	10
1325 – 1126 B.C.	+150	1499–1250 B.C.	4
1550 – 1326 B.C.	+200	1749–1500 B.C.	9
1750 – 1551 B.C.	+200	1999–1750 B.C.	6
1900 – 1751 B.C.	+300	2249–2000 B.C.	12
2050 – 1900 B.C.	+400	2499–2250 B.C.	4
2225 – 2051 B.C.	+500	2749–2500 B.C.	6
2450 – 2226 B.C.	+550	2999–2750 B.C.	6
2650 – 2451 B.C.	+550	3249–3000 B.C.	7
2850 – 2651 B.C.	+650	3499–3250 B.C.	5
[3700 – 2951 B.C.]	+700	[4395–3645 B.C.] (750 years)	11
[4366 – 4060 B.C.]	+750	[5116–4810 B.C.] (306 years)	9
		Total	176

* + = C¹⁴ dates are younger than calendar dates by the number of years indicated. − = C¹⁴ dates are older than calendar dates by the number of years indicated.

Exercise 35

Variability in Fossil Populations

One of the major problems of interpretation of the fossil record is the determination of the range of variability within a *paleospecies*. Is a particular specimen typical of the population? Are two specimens within the range of variation for a particular paleo-species?

PROBLEMS

Following are two sets of data, the first for Neandertal fossils, the second for early *H. sapiens sapiens* fossils. Each chart gives the maximum length of the skull (max. lgth.), maximum breadth of the skull (max. br.), *cranial index* (C.I.), and *cranial capacity* (cran. cap.). The cranial index is calculated

$$\frac{\text{max. br.}}{\text{max. lgth.}} \times 100$$

Take one of the characteristics. For both Neandertals and early moderns, cal-culate the *mean* and *standard deviation* (see Exercise 15). Next, calculate the mean and standard deviation for each of the other characteristics. Then answer the following questions:

1. By how much do the means differ between the two groups for each characteristic? For which feature does this difference appear to be the greatest? The least? (Think of the difference in terms of percent difference.)

218

Find	Location	Max. Lgth. (mm)	Max. Br. (mm)	C.I.	Cran. Cap. (cc)
		Neandertals			
Broken Hill	Rhodesia	208	144.5	69.5	1,280
Gibraltar	Gibraltar	192	144	75.0	1,200
Jebel Irhoud	Morocco	200	146	73.0	1,500
La Chapelle-aux-Saints	France	208	156	75.0	Over 1,600*
La Ferrassie I	France	209	158	75.6	1,641
Le Moustier	France	196	150	76.5	1,350
Monte Circeo I	Italy	204	156	76.5	1,550
Neandertal	Germany	199	147	73.9	1,450
Saccopastore I	Italy	182	142	78.0	1,200
Saldanha	S. Africa	200	144	72.0	1,200−1,250*
Skhul V	Israel	192	144	75.0	1,450−1,518*
Spy I	Belgium	202	144	71.3	
Spy II	Belgium	198	150	75.8	
Tabūn I	Israel	183	141	77.0	
		Early Modern			
Boskop	S. Africa	205	154	75.1	
Brünn I	Moravia	206	144	69.9	1,600?*
Cape Flats	S. Africa	191	132	69.1	
Chancelade	France	193	139	72.0	1,530
Chatelperron	France	186	158	84.9	
Choukoutien 101	China	204	143	70.1	1,500
Choukoutien 102	China	196	140	71.4	1,380
Choukoutien 103	China	184	133	72.3	1,300
Cohuna	Australia	199	131	65.8	1,260?*
Combe Capelle	France	198	130	65.7	1,440
Cro-Magnon	France	202.5	149.5	73.8	1,590
Fish Hoek	S. Africa	200	150	75.0	1,600
Gamble's Cave M	Kenya	200	130	65.0	
Gamble's Cave F	Kenya	190	144	75.8	
Ingwavuma	S. Africa	200	140	70.0	1,450
Liu Kwang	China	189	142	75.1	1,480
Oberkassel	Germany	194	144	74.2	1,500
Predmost 3	Czechoslovakia	202	145	71.8	1,580
Oredmost 4	Czechoslovakia	181	127	70.2	1,250
Springbok	S. Africa	195	144	73.8	1,540
Wadjak	Java	200	145	72.5	1,593

*Exclude in calculations.

Source: Data for max. lgth., max. br., and cran. cap. from T. W. Phenice, *Hominid Fossils: An Illustrated Key* (Dubuque, Iowa: Wm. C. Brown, 1972).

Variability in Fossil Populations

2. For each feature, is the variability, as measured by the standard deviation, greater in the Neandertal population or in the modern population?

3. Does the mean for the Neandertal population for any feature fall within the range of variation of the modern population? What about the reverse? How much overlap is there between the two populations? (You might want to illustrate this overlap diagrammatically or on a graph.)

ANSWERS
1. Neandertals

Max. lgth.	$N = 14$	$\overline{X} = 198.1$	$s = 8.5$
Max. br.	$N = 14$	$\overline{X} = 147.6$	$s = 5.5$
C.I.	$N = 14$	$\overline{X} = 74.6$	$s = 2.4$
Cran. cap.	$N = 8*$	$\overline{X} = 1396$	$s = 165$

Early Modern

Max. lgth.	$N = 21$	$\overline{X} = 196.0$	$s = 7.0$
Max. br.	$N = 21$	$\overline{X} = 141.2$	$s = 8.3$
C.I.	$N = 21$	$\overline{X} = 72.1$	$s = 4.3$
Cran. cap.	$N = 14*$	$\overline{X} = 1481$	$s = 109$

*Only cranial capacities of which a single determination (without a question mark) is given were used.

Exercise 36

Recognizing Fossil Hominids

The family Hominidae is divided by paleoanthropologists into several genera and paleospecies. However, the purpose of this exercise is not to deal with problems of classification but to develop a familiarity with some of the fossil forms through the examination of casts. Although photographs are reproduced here, it is hoped that the actual casts are available. In addition, it is hoped that fossils other than the four presented here can also be studied.

PROBLEM
Figures 36-1 and 36-2 show the front and side view of *A. africanus, H. erectus* (Choukoutien), *H. sapiens neandertalensis* (La Chapelle-aux-Saints), and *H. sapiens sapiens* (Choukoutien). Following is a chart of several features of the skull. Compare each feature for each skull and describe its characteristics in the appropriate column.

SUGGESTED READINGS
Day, M. *Guide to Fossil Man: A Handbook of Human Palaeontology.* Cleveland: World, 1965.

Phenice, T. W. *Hominid Fossils: An Illustrated Key.* Dubuque, Iowa: Wm. C. Brown, 1972.

Pilbeam, D. R. *The Ascent of Man: An Introduction to Human Evolution.* New York: Macmillan, 1972.

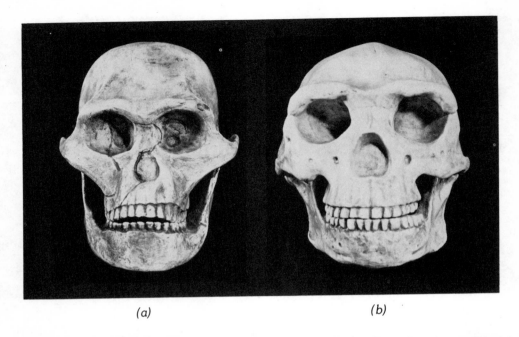

(a)

(b)

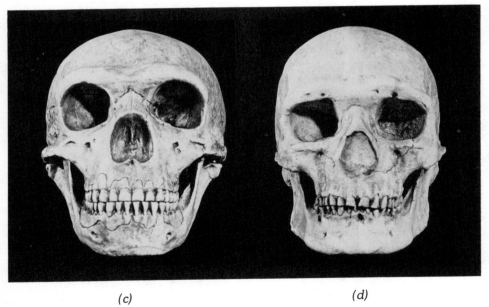

(c)

(d)

Figure 36-1 Front views of (a) *Australopithecus africanus*, (b) *Homo erectus*, (c) *Homo sapiens neandertalensis*, (d) *Homo sapiens sapiens*.

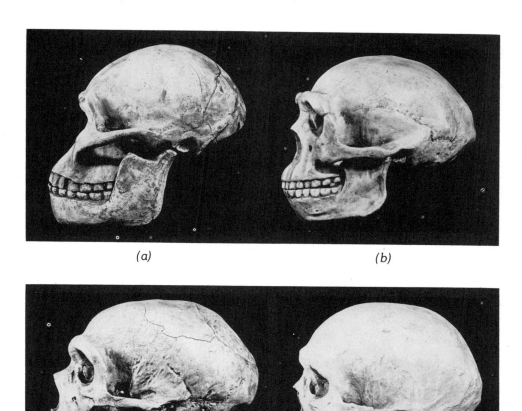

(a) *(b)*

(c) *(d)*

Figure 36-2 Side views of (a) *Australopithecus africanus,* (b) *Homo erectus,* (c) *Homo sapiens neandertalensis,* (d) *Homo sapiens sapiens.*

Features of the Skull

Feature	A. africanus	H. erectus	H. sapiens neandertalensis	H. sapiens sapiens
Shape of brain case				
Forehead				
Occipital region				
Development of brow ridge				
Prognathism of face				
Relative size of facial skeleton				
Relative thickness of zygomatic arch				
Presence of chin				
Size of jaw relative to cranium				
Other significant features				

Exercise 37

Osteometry of Fossil Skulls

Many of the changes which have occurred in hominid evolution have been changes in proportions of the skull. This is most noticeable when we examine the progressive enlargement of the brain case, the progressive reduction of the facial skeleton, and the more central positioning of the occipital condyles on the base of the skull. These trends will be illustrated in this exercise by a series of measurements and indices. Ideally, measurements should be taken on actual casts, but for our purposes we will utilize a series of outline drawings showing several skulls from the side.

Before taking measurements, we must locate several points on the skull and draw in a number of lines. These will be illustrated on a series of line drawings of a modern human skull.

Figure 37-1 shows a modern human skull with a number of points identified. These points are:

1. The *porion,* which is the highest point on the margin of the *external auditory meatus.*

2. The position of the *occipital condyles.* Since these cannot be seen in side view, their position has been marked with an arrow.

3. The lowest point on the facial skeleton between the two medial incisors is the *prosthion.*

4. Two points should be marked on the orbit, the lowest point and the highest point.

5. The highest point on the skull should be indicated.

6. The *inion* is the point on the back of the skull which is the greatest distance away from the front of the skull.

After the above points are located, a series of lines are drawn in as shown in Figure 37-2.

1. It is important that all skulls be oriented in the same way. In osteometric studies skulls are usually oriented in what is called the *Frankfort plane*. In this orientation a horizontal line, parallel to the top of the page, should intersect the porion and the lowest point on the lower margin of the orbit.

2. Draw a line from the highest point on the skull, which we label point v, perpendicular to the Frankfort plane. The point at which this line intersects the Frankfort plane is labeled t.

3. Draw a line from the inion perpendicular to the Frankfort plane. The point of intersection is labeled y.

4. Draw a line up from the occipital condyles (indicated by the arrow) perpendicular to the Frankfort plane. The point of intersection is labeled x.

5. Draw a line up from the prosthion perpendicular to the Frankfort plane. The point of intersection is labeled z.

6. Draw a line parallel to the Frankfort plane from the highest point on the upper margin of the orbit. The intersection of this line with the line from v to t is labeled u.

7. Draw a line parallel to the Frankfort plane from the inion. The intersection of this line with the line from v to t is labeled w.

The following measurements are then taken. Do not attach any great importance to the measurements of the various skulls, since they are not all drawn to the same scale. Identical scale is not important in this exercise, since we will be dealing with indices.

1. Measure the length of the line from u to v.
2. Measure the length of the line from t to v.
3. Measure the length of the line from t to w.
4. Measure the length of the line from x to y.
5. Measure the length of the line from x to z.

From the measurements the following three indices are calculated:

1. Index of supraorbital height $= \dfrac{uv}{tv} \times 100$

2. Index of nuchal area height $= \dfrac{tw}{tv} \times 100$

3. Index of condylar position $= \dfrac{xy}{xz} \times 100$

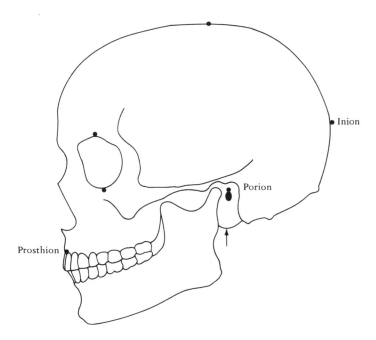

Figure 37-1 A modern human skull. This figure shows the points which are to be located on all skulls in this exercise.

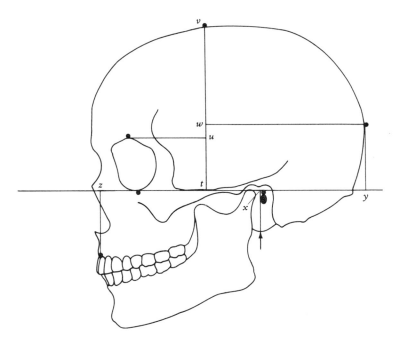

Figure 37-2 A modern human skull. This figure shows the lines which are to be drawn on all skulls in this exercise.

PROBLEMS

1. Figure 37-3 is a series of outlines of skulls. For each skull locate the proper points, draw in the lines and take the measurements, and then calculate the three indices. The measurements and indices are to be placed on the chart on page 233.

2. On the graph, locate the point where the lines from the index of supraorbital height and index of nuchal area height intersect for each skull. Label each point.

3. How would you interpret the data on the chart and graph? What conclusions can you make about the general trends in hominid evolution as reflected in these skulls?

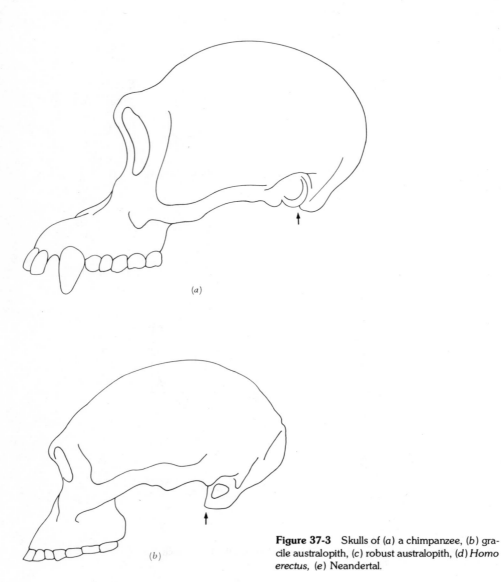

(a)

(b)

Figure 37-3 Skulls of (a) a chimpanzee, (b) gracile australopith, (c) robust australopith, (d) *Homo erectus*, (e) Neandertal.

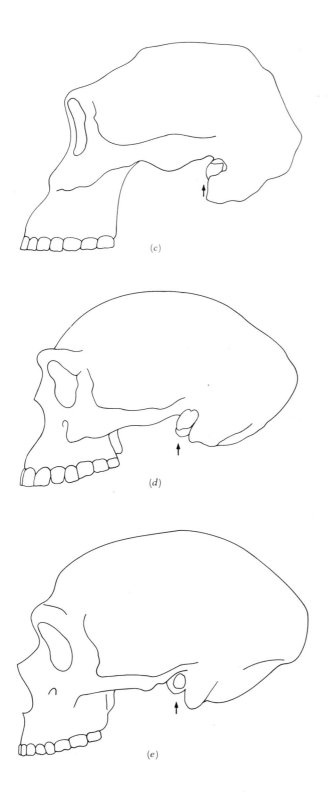

(c)

(d)

(e)

ANSWERS

Skull	Index of Supraorbital Height	Index of Nuchal Area Height	Index of Condylar Position
Chimpanzee	47	31	24
Gracile australopith	72	34	51
Robust australopith	48	19	53
H. erectus	56	25	80
Neandertal	66	39	81
Modern H. sapiens	68	41	67

Skull	u-v	t-v	t-w	x-y	x-z	Index of Supraorbital Height	Index of Nuchal Area Height	Index of Condylar Position
Chimpanzee								
Gracile australopith								
Robust australopith								
H. erectus								
Neandertal								
Modern H. sapiens								

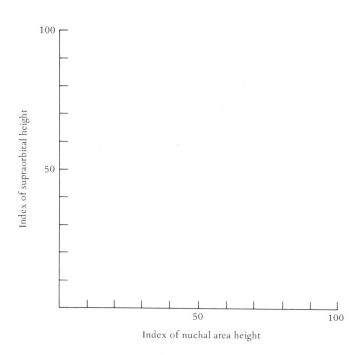

Glossary

Words which are italicized in a glossary entry are defined under their own entry.

Absolute dating A method of dating that gives a specific point in time that can be located in relationship to a specific calendar system. See *radiometric dating.*

Agglutination Clumping of *cells* as a result of an *antigen-antibody* reaction.

Albinism A genetic abnormality, inherited as a *recessive,* characterized by a lack of melanin (skin pigment) production.

Alkaptonuria A genetic abnormality, inherited as a *recessive,* characterized by a darkening of urine when exposed to light; a form of arthritis.

Allele An alternate form of a specific *gene.*

Anterior Toward the front of the body.

Anthropometry The study of the measurements of the human body.

Antibody A protein produced by the body, usually in the presence of an *antigen.* Antibodies react with and neutralize *antigens.*

Antigen A substance foreign to an organism which stimulates the production or action of *antibodies* within that organism.

Assortative mating Nonrandom mate selection; preference or avoidance of individuals for physical, social, or cultural reasons.

Atom The basic building block of matter. Atoms are made up of three basic subatomic units: *protons* and *neutrons* (except for hydrogen 1, which has no neutrons) in the *nucleus* and one or more electrons that orbit the nucleus. There are ninety-two naturally occurring types of atoms, including carbon, oxygen, hydrogen, and nitrogen.

Attached earlobes A trait, inherited as a *recessive,* in which the lower part of the ear attaches directly onto the head. See *free-hanging earlobes.*

Attribute A distinctive quality or characteristic that can be used to describe or classify a fossil, artifact, people, time period, and so on.

Balanced polymorphism Maintenance of a stable relationship between two or more alleles of a given gene in a population where at least two of the alleles have frequencies greater than 1 percent. One form of balanced polymorphism results from *selection* in favor of the *heterozygous genotype.*

Bipedalism Upright posture and habitual movement on two legs.

Blastula Early embryonic stage characterized by a hollow ball of *cells.*

Blood-type system A group of *polymorphic* blood proteins determined by a single *gene* or a set of closely *linked genes.*

Brachiation A form of locomotion whereby the animal suspends itself by its arms and moves hand over hand.

Brachydactyly A genetic skeletal abnormality, inherited as a *dominant,* characterized by very short fingers.

Brown tooth enamel A genetic abnormality, inherited as an *X-linked dominant,* characterized by defective tooth enamel, resulting in brown teeth.

Calvaria That portion of the skull which houses the brain.

Cartilage An elastic tissue that in *vertebrates* is the main skeletal element in embryos and in most vertebrates is ultimately converted into bone in most parts of the adult skeleton.

Catarrhine nose A nose form in which the nostrils are spaced close together, separated by a narrow nasal septum, with nasal openings pointing downward; found in Old World monkeys, apes, and humans.

Cell The smallest unit which is considered to be alive. All living organisms are either one cell or composed of several cells.

Centriole A pair of small bodies found near the nucleus of the cell from which the *spindle fibers* radiate.

Centromere Part of a *chromosome;* a constriction which "ties" two *chromatids* together.

Chondrodystrophic dwarfism A genetic abnormality, inherited as a *dominant,* characterized by a normal-sized head and trunk but very short limbs.

Chordate A member of the phylum Chordata; characterized by the presence of a *notochord; dorsal,* single, hollow nerve cord; and gill slits at some point in the life cycle.

Chromatid A chromosomal strand; a complete *chromosome* consists of a pair of chromatids.

Chromosomal aberration An abnormality of the *chromosomes;* either an abnormal number or some type of structural abnormality.

Chromosome A body found within the *nucleus* of the *cell* which contains the hereditary material.

Codominance The situation in which, in the *heterozygous* condition, both *alleles* are expressed in the *phenotype*.

Color-blindness A genetic abnormality, several forms of which are inherited as X-linked recessives. It is characterized by the inability to distinguish between certain colors, or in one non-X-linked form, the inability to see color at all.

Congenital aniridia Absence of the iris of the eye.

Congenital deafness Deafness present at birth.

Consanguineous mating Mating between biologically related individuals.

Cranial capacity The volume of the brain case (not the size of the brain itself).

Cranium The skull minus the *mandible*.

Culture Learned, symbolic, nonrandom, systematic behavior that can be transmitted from individual to individual and from generation to generation.

Cytoplasm Material within the *cell* between the cell membrane and the *nucleus*.

Dental comb A structure found in lemurs and lorises, used, in part, in grooming, consisting of the lower canines and incisors projecting forward almost horizontally.

Dental formula Formal designation of types and number of teeth. The dental formula of $\frac{2.1.2.3}{2.1.2.3}$ indicates that in one-half of the upper jaw and one-half of the lower jaw there are two incisors, one canine, two premolars, and three molars.

Dermatoglyphics The study of *epidermal ridges*.

Diaphysis The growth center of the mid-portion of the shaft of a long bone.

Diastema Spaces in the upper and lower jaws of monkeys and apes into which the canines of the opposite jaw fit when the mouth is closed.

Diploid Refers to the full complement of chromosomes, forty-six in humans, found in all *cells* except *gametes*.

Displacement In relationship to *dominance hierarchies,* a situation in which one animal can cause another to move away from food, a sitting spot, and so on.

Diurnal Active during the daylight hours.

Dizygotic twins Twins originating from two separate *zygotes* (fraternal twins).

Dominance hierarchy A system of social ranking within an animal group, based upon *displacement* and other unequal interactions.

Dominant The allele which is expressed in the *heterozygous* individual.

Dorsal Toward the top or back of an animal.

Epidermal ridges Sensory ridges found on the fingertips, palms, soles of the feet, and toes.

Epiphyseal union The growing together and fusion of the *diaphysis* and *epiphysis*.

Epiphysis   The growth center at either end of a bone.

Estrus   The period of sexual receptivity in the female.

Fertility   The number of births during a specific time period for a particular population.

Fitness   The measure of how well an individual or group is adapted to a specific environment.

Folk taxonomy   Classification of any group of objects, people, or events, based on cultural tradition.

Forensic science   The study of any material, including measurement of human remains, to obtain evidence admissible in criminal or military court proceedings.

Free-hanging earlobes   A genetic trait, inherited as a *dominant,* where the earlobe hangs free as opposed to being attached. See *attached earlobes.*

Gamete   A *haploid sex cell* produced by *meiosis.* In a bisexual animal species, the sex cell is either a *sperm* or an *ovum.*

Gene   A chromosomal segment with a specific function.

Gene pool   The sum of all alleles of all individuals within a population.

Genetic drift   A chance deviation in gene frequencies from one generation to the next in a *gene pool* which is due to finite population size.

Genetic equilibrium   A situation in which *allele* frequencies remain constant from generation to generation.

Genotype   The genetic constitution of an individual.

Giemsa staining   A method of staining *chromosomes* which results in a distinctive banding pattern for each chromosome pair.

Glucose-6-phosphate dehydrogenase deficiency   An *X-linked recessive* trait characterized by a severe anemia when the individual is in contact with the fava bean or certain antimalarial drugs.

Grooming   Going through the fur, removing parasites and other matter such as twigs, burrs, or dirt; also serves as an expression of close social ties.

Haploid   Refers to the complement of *chromosomes,* twenty-three in humans, found in the *gametes.*

Hardy-Weinberg formula   A mathematical expression of *genetic equilibrium:* $p^2 + 2pq + q^2 = 1.$

Hemoglobin   The red pigment (protein) found in the red *cells* of the blood which functions to transport oxygen.

Hemophilia   A *recessive X-linked* trait characterized by excessive bleeding due to a faulty clotting mechanism.

Heterodonty   Having different types of teeth in each region of the jaws for different functions (tearing, cutting, grinding).

Heterozygous   Possessing two different *alleles* of a particular *gene.*

Homologous chromosomes   *Chromosomes* of the same pair.

Homozygous Possessing two like *alleles* of a particular *gene;* called homozygous dominant when the alleles are *dominant* and homozygous recessive when the alleles are *recessive.*

Huntington's chorea A genetic abnormality, inherited as a *dominant,* characterized by a breakdown of the nervous system, leading to death. Age of onset is variable but averages about thirty-five years.

Ichthyosis A genetic abnormality, inherited as an *X-linked recessive,* involving the scaling of the skin beginning at birth.

Independent assortment The concept that different genes are inherited independently of one another.

Inspection method As applied to aging and sexing of skeletal remains, the determination of age and sex by visual observations, as opposed to measurements.

Intermembral index A measure of the relative length of the arms and legs on the skeleton: $\dfrac{\text{humerus + radius}}{\text{femur + tibia}} \times 100$.

Ischial callosities A pair of calluses on the buttocks of some Old World monkeys and apes.

Karyotype A standardized classification and arrangement of *chromosomes.*

Linked genes *Genes* located on the same chromosome.

Mammals The class of the phylum Chordata (*chordates*) characterized by a constant level of activity independent of external temperature; mammary glands; hair or fur; *heterodonty;* and other features.

Mandible The lower jaw.

Mean The arithmetic average.

Meiosis The form of *cell* division occurring in specialized tissue in the testes and ovaries, leading to the production of *gametes.*

Mitosis The form of *cell* division whereby one-celled organisms divide and whereby body cells divide in growth and replacement.

Monozygotic twins Identical twins derived from a single *zygote.*

Mortality In its biostatistical sense, the number of deaths during a specific period of time for a specific population.

Mounting A behavioral pattern whereby one animal jumps upon the *posterior* area of a second animal as a part of the act of copulation or as a dominance display.

Mutation A change in the genetic material.

Mutation rate The number of mutations per *gene* per *gamete* per generation.

Nasal index A measure of the breadth of the nose as compared with the height of the nose: $\dfrac{\text{nasal breadth}}{\text{nasal height}} \times 100$.

Natural selection   Changes in *allelic* frequencies in a population resulting from differences in *fertility* and *mortality* among individuals with different *genotypes*.

Neutron   A particle found in the *nucleus* of an *atom*; neutrons have no electric charge. See *proton*.

Notochord   The rod made of cartilage along the *dorsal* side of the body; characteristic of all *chordates* at some point in their life cycle.

Nuclear membrane   The membrane which binds off the *nucleus* of a *cell*.

Nucleus (of an atom)   The central portion of an *atom*, composed of *protons* and, with the exception of hydrogen 1, *neutrons*.

Nucleus (of a cell)   The part of the *cell*, bounded by the *nuclear membrane*, which contains the *chromosomes*.

Olfactory   Referring to the sense of smell.

Ontogeny   The study of growth and development from conception to death.

Ossification   The formation of bone.

Osteological   Of or relating to bone.

Osteometry   The study of the measurements of skeletal material.

Ovum   Female *gamete*.

Paleospecies   A population of fossils whose range of variation does not exceed the range of variation found within a closely related modern *species*.

Pedigree   A reconstruction of the matings within a family group that have taken place over the generations.

Phenotype   The sum of an organism's observable or measurable characteristics; one specific trait.

Phenylketonuria   An abnormality in the metabolism of the amino acid phenylalanine, leading to severe mental retardation; inherited as a *recessive*.

Phylum   A major division of a kingdom (such as Animalia) that represents a basic body plan. See *chordate*.

Platyrrhine nose   A nose form in which the nostrils are usually separated by a broad nasal septum and in which the nostrils open sideways; characteristic of the New World monkeys.

Polar body   The small *cells* resulting from the unequal division of the *cytoplasm* in *meiosis* in the female.

Polymorphism   The presence of several distinct forms of a *gene* or a phenotypic trait within a population.

Population   A group of organisms which is potentially capable of successful reproduction (also called a reproductive or Mendelian population).

Postcranial skeleton   The skeleton, excluding the skull.

Posterior   Near the rear of the body.

Prehensile tail   A tail which is capable of picking up objects and supporting the body when hanging from a branch.

Primates   The order of the class Mammalia (*mammals*) which includes the *prosimians,* monkeys, apes, and humans.

Proband   The individual on whose behalf a *pedigree* is constructed.

Prosimians   Primates who are members of the suborder Prosimii, the "lower primates," including the lemurs, lorises, and tarsiers.

Proton   A particle, bearing a positive charge, found in the *nucleus* of an *atom.* See *neutron.*

Quadrupedalism   Movement on four limbs.

Radial symmetry   A type of body plan in which the parts of the body are arranged in a more or less regular manner around a center.

Radiocarbon dating   A *radiometric dating* technique based on the decay of radioactive carbon 14.

Radiometric dating   Any of the *absolute dating* methods based on the decay of radioactive *atoms.*

Recessive   The state of an *allele* that is not expressed in the *heterozygous* individual.

Relative fitness   The degree of difference in *fertility* and *mortality* rates among various *genotypes* with respect to a particular *gene.*

Retinoblastoma   A hereditary cancer of the *eye,* inherited as a *recessive.*

Sampling error   Deviation from an expected frequency due to small population size.

Scent-marking   Marking territory by urine or feces or by rubbing scent glands against trees or other objects.

Selection   See *natural selection.*

Semibrachiation   Extensive use of hands and/or *prehensile tail* in forms otherwise *quadrupedal.*

Serum   The liquid portion of the blood from which the clotting factors have been removed.

Sex cell   A *gamete.*

Sex-influenced trait   A characteristic which is the result of an *allele* whose *phenotypic* expression differs in males and females.

Sex linkage   Traits being inherited on the *X* or *Y chromosomes.*

Sexual dimorphism   Observable or measurable differences in size and body structure between males and females of a *species.*

Sexual skin   A naked area on the buttocks of a female monkey or ape which swells and changes color when the animal is in *estrus.*

Sickle-cell anemia   Severe anemia caused by the presence of *hemoglobin* S in place of hemoglobin A. In the *homozygous* individual the red blood cells assume a sickle shape during recurring crises.

Sickle-cell trait   A condition in which red blood cells contain both *hemoglobin* A and S but cells do not sickle in crises. (See *Sickle-cell anemia.*)

Site In archaeology, the scene of previous human activity.

Somatic cells Body or nonsex *cells*.

Species The largest natural *population* whose members are potentially able to reproduce successfully among themselves, but not with members of other species.

Sperm Male *gamete*.

Spindle fibers A structure consisting of fibers radiating out from the *centrioles* which attach to the *centromere* in *cell* division.

Standard deviation A measurement of variation: $s = \sqrt{\dfrac{\Sigma x^2}{N-1}}$.

Standard error of the mean Measurement of the reliability of a sample: $s_{\bar{x}} = \dfrac{s}{\sqrt{N}}$.

Taxonomy The study of classification.

Tongue folding The ability to turn the tip of the tongue back upon the body of the tongue without using the teeth in any way; inherited as a *recessive*.

Tongue rolling The ability to roll the tongue longitudinally into a U shape; inherited as a *dominant*.

Vertebrate A major division of the phylum Chordata (*chordates*) which includes animals with a segmented vertebral column (spine).

Vertical clinging and leaping A method of movement in which the animal clings vertically to a branch and moves between branches by leaping vertically from one to another.

X chromosome In humans, one of the group C *chromosomes*. Normal females possess two and normal males possess one in each body *cell*.

X-linked Located on the *X chromosome*.

Xg blood-type system A *blood-type system* based upon the presence or absence of the Xg *antigen*; inherited as an *X-linked recessive*.

Y chromosome In humans, one of the group G *chromosomes*, found in males only, which appears to influence the development of a human as a male.

Y-linked Located on the *Y chromosome*.

Zygote The fertilized *ovum*.